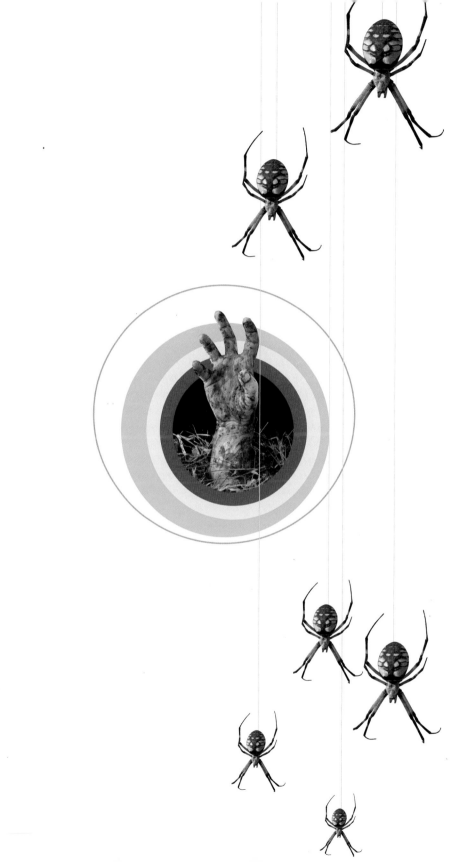

That's CREEPY!

BY CRISPIN BOYER

NATIONAL GEOGRAPHIC
WASHINGTON, D.C.

CREEPY Contents

Meet Your Creepy Co-Hosts!

Meet Your Creepy Co-Hosts!

AGENT JEEPER THE G-MAN

HEY, KIDDO. I'M SPECIAL AGENT JEEPER OF THE CIA—you know, the Creepy Intelligence Agency—and I come bearing a warning: Don't read this book before bedtime! Inside you'll find a history of bloodthirsty monsters, tales of infamous phantoms, and purported proof of the paranormal. No spooky subject goes unexplored! It's enough to give you nightmares if you let it, and that's where I come in. As someone who's spent his career investigating oddball phenomena and chasing creepy creatures, I can assure you this supernatural stuff is a bunch of hooey! Bigfoot? A dude in a suit! Ghosts? Figments of your imagination! Flying saucers? Don't even get me started!

Consider ol' Agent Jeeper your voice of reason as you creep through chapter after spooky chapter of *That's Creepy!* If you come across something that makes you feel faint with fright, don't panic! I'll be on hand with a "reality check" that offers a rational explanation for the terrible topic at hand. By the end of the book, you'll be a certified skeptic!

ETHEL THE E.T.

GREETINGS, EARTHLING. MY NAME IS [UNPRONOUNCEABLE SCREECH], BUT YOU CAN CALL ME ETHEL. I'm what you'd call an extraterrestrial, meaning I'm not from around these parts…or even this solar system. My home's nice enough, I suppose. We have two suns, six moons, and 79.3 hours of round-the-clock daylight thanks to our fancy-schmancy orbital solar reflectors. But if there's a downside to living in a hyper-advanced interplanetary civilization with no nightlife, it's that everything is so bright and shiny and safe. Frankly, it's a little boring.

Not like here! With all of your horror movies, campfire ghost stories, and bone-chilling legends of terrifying monsters, you Earthlings aren't afraid to scare yourselves silly. Hey, a little bit of fright can be fun, right? That's why I've been coming here for centuries, commuting across the light-years to study the creepy side of Earth's culture. I've become a true believer in your fearsome folklore and supernatural stories. Look for me to share bonus bits of "disturbing data" throughout the book. Until then, I gotta fly!

BOO! ~

CIA

How to Get the Most From
That's CREEPY!

The stomach tightens, senses heighten, muscles grow taut—these are familiar sensations for anyone who has watched a scary movie or trundled up the first hill of a roller coaster. They're the symptoms of fear, an automatic response that puts your body into instant alert, and they're actually crucial to your survival. Without a healthy sense of fear, you might mosey off a mountaintop or leap into the ocean to pet a passing shark. So don't try to suppress those spine tingles as you peruse *That's Creepy!* They're part of an essential instinct!

STEP 2: KNOW YOUR TERRIBLE TERMINOLOGY!

This book is full of terms that don't pop up in your everyday life. If you're stumped about the meaning of a word, flip back to this glossary.

APPARITION: A ghost that appears in a visible form, often as a human-shaped figure.

COVEN: A gathering of witches, usually in groups of 13.

CRYPTID: A legendary or "hidden" creature, such as Bigfoot or the Loch Ness Monster.

CRYPTOZOOLOGY: The study of cryptids, practiced by cryptozoologists.

FOLKLORE: Tales and legends passed down over time.

HAUNTING: A ghost making its presence known in a particular location.

HYSTERIA: An unstoppable sense of fear and panic that spreads from person to person.

LYCANTHROPY: The ability to transform into a wolf.

PARANORMAL: Phenomena beyond the boundaries of science or what's considered "normal."

PARAPSYCHOLOGY: The study of mental powers.

SPECTER: Another name for a ghost (along with phantom, spirit, and spook).

VAMPIRE: Dead beings that survive by drinking the blood of the living.

STEP 3: GET READY TO RATE!

Agent Jeeper and Ethel the E.T. rarely agree, but they both know creepy when they see it! The two teamed up to create the PhEAR Factor—a meter for measuring abnormal reactions to scary phenomena. The higher something ranks on this scale, the creepier it is! You'll find PhEAR Factors at the end of each chapter. Disagree? Make your own!

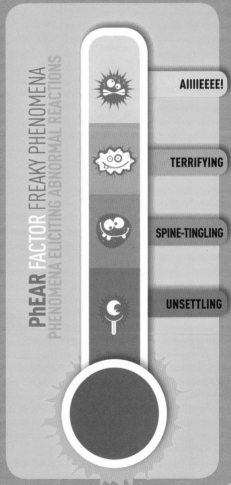

PhEAR FACTOR FREAKY PHENOMENA
PHENOMENA ELICITING ABNORMAL REACTIONS

AIIIIEEEE!

TERRIFYING

SPINE-TINGLING

UNSETTLING

Run to
the
LIGHT!

It's a Frightening Fact!

Feelings of fear invoke physical responses, including increased heart rate, goose bumps on your skin, and the release of a chemical called adrenaline that puts your body on edge. If you feel faint with fright or just need a nightlight while reading this book, retreat to this page for a blast of comforting daylight—the enemy of all things creepy! We suggest you bookmark this fright-free refuge and make frequent rest stops as you plumb the inner reaches of *That's Creepy!*

CHAPTER 1

Bloodsuckers

THEY PREEN. THEY POUT. THEY SPARKLE IN THE SUNLIGHT. Today's movie and TV vampires are more pretty than creepy, especially compared with their moon-pale predecessors from folklore and fiction. To experience the pure terror of these hematophagous (or blood-drinking) horrors, we must plunge back to the bone-chilling basics of the vampire legend—back to when the myth still had teeth! Order a pizza with extra garlic as we unearth the origins of Count Dracula, dodge bloodsucking bats, and meet a modern-day creature of the night!

THE GORY STORY OF VAMPIRES

STORIES of supernatural creatures guzzling the blood of the living are common in many cultures going back to ancient times. The Romans feared the stryx, an owl-like demon that feasted on human flesh. Romanians were wary of strigoi, restless spirits that rose from the grave to feed on the living. People in the Philippines scanned the night skies for the manananggal, a human-shaped fiend with a gruesome gimmick: Its winged torso could rip free from its lower body to soar above villages, where it slurped the blood of children through a dangling straw-like tongue. The list of blood-gobblers goes on. Pick a place and period in the past, and the locals will share tales of creatures out for blood. Imagine contemplating such frights each night before the invention of the night-light!

Amid the plagues and superstitions of medieval Europe rose the fear of revenants (from the French word for "return"). These walking corpses stake the strongest claim to the modern vampire myth. Hardly the suave, sharply dressed bloodsuckers we know today, revenants were pudgy, slack-jawed peasants who tormented family members and neighbors before returning to their graves, mouths messy with blood. The word "vampire"—from the Serbian term *vampir*—entered the English language in the 1700s after appearing in official reports of revenant stakings.

Drawing from this fearsome folklore and historical facts, Irish novelist Bram Stoker concocted a tale of the most famous vampire of all in 1897. His Transylvanian terror, Count Dracula, gave new life to the bloodthirsty undead.

GRAVE CONSEQUENCES

According to modern myth, only the bite of a vampire can make another vampire. Folklore, however, offers lots of entry points for wannabe bloodsuckers, including …

Original Fangsters

LILITH (CIRCA 2000 B.C., MESOPOTAMIA)

The mother of all bloodsuckers, this winged Sumerian demon preyed upon infants in the night, snatching them in their sleep with her talons. Her legendary bloodthirstiness inspired vampire folklore.

PETER PLOGOJOWITZ (CIRCA A.D. 1725, EASTERN EUROPE)

Weeks after his death, this Serbian farmer was blamed for draining several people in his village. Vampire folklore was a fact of life by this time, so the villagers knew what to do when they dug up Plogojowitz's corpse and discovered fresh blood trickling from his mouth. They drove a stake through his heart.

LAMIA (CIRCA 600 B.C., ANCIENT GREECE)

Transformed into a snake-tailed creature after she chugged the blood of children, this former girlfriend of the Greek god Zeus began preying on men instead, draining their veins until they withered and perished.

 ...drinking milk from a cow that was once the victim of a vampire

 ...getting in trouble with the church

 ...being the seventh child in your family

 ...being born on Christmas

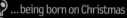 ...having an animal jump over your dead body

PRINCE *Harm*

Meet the Bloodthirsty Ruler Who Inspired Dracula

AS THE SUN DIPS BEHIND THE CRAGS OF THE CARPATHIAN MOUNTAINS, A DAMP CHILL GRIPS THE DARK FORESTS, CRUMBLING CASTLES, AND SCATTERED VILLAGES OF CENTRAL ROMANIA. The misty landscape is eerily silent . . . until the wolves begin to howl. It's no wonder author Bram Stoker chose this region—known as Transylvania—as Count Dracula's home turf. But "the land beyond the forest" contributed more than just creepy scenery for his famous novel. It's also the birthplace of a 15th-century Romanian prince named Vlad III, aka Vlad Dracula.

No sweet prince, Vlad was a ruthless warlord who fought dirty to defend his father's territory of Wallachia, a region south of Transylvania. He once marched plague victims into enemy encampments to spread a deadly infection—an early case of biological warfare. But Vlad's greatest weapon was fear, which he spread through an especially gruesome method of torturing enemies to death. Vlad reportedly impaled tens of thousands of enemies on "forests" of stakes. He even feasted among his victims. When a dinner guest complained about the rotten stink, an outraged Vlad offered just deserts: He fetched the tallest stake and had the whiny diner impaled above the rest.

Today, Vlad Dracula is known as Vlad Tepes, or "Vlad the Impaler." Although he was never accused of drinking blood in his day (those stories came later), Vlad struck a sinister chord with Bram Stoker. The prince's name—and possibly his legendary bloodlust—served as inspiration for the character of Count Dracula, as did the Transylvanian "old country" in which Vlad was born.

Romanian prince Vlad Dracula's nickname translates to "son of the dragon" (his father was named Dracul after joining the special Order of the Dragon). The word "Dracula" also means "son of the devil."

ing

OTHER FAMOUS FICTIONAL FIENDS

THE GOOD: EDWARD CULLEN (FROM THE TWILIGHT SERIES OF BOOKS)

This pouty teenage vampire falls in love with a human girl named Bella Swan and must protect her from his evil kin. Too much of a bleeding heart to drink human blood, Cullen feeds only on animals. *SPECIAL POWER:* Cullen can mosey around in broad daylight. Instead of burning him, the sun makes his skin sparkle.

THE BAD: LORD RUTHVEN (FROM THE 1819 SHORT STORY "THE VAMPYRE")

Before Bram Stoker unleashed Dracula, this dapper vampire infiltrated London society and drank the blood of women—including the sister of a friend. What a bloodthirsty jerk! *SPECIAL POWER:* As the star of the first English vampire tale, Ruthven established the enduring image of these nocturnal creatures as fashionable and charming immortal noblemen.

THE CREEPY: THE MASTER (FROM THE TV SERIES *BUFFY THE VAMPIRE SLAYER*)

This ancient and ugly creature is the Drac daddy of a vampire cult in Sunnydale, the fictional hometown of cheerleader-turned-bloodsucker-slayer Buffy Summers. *SPECIAL POWER:* The Master intends to open a hellish portal beneath Sunnydale High School—unless Buffy can serve him "stake" first.

THE CREEPIEST: COUNT ORLOK
(FROM THE 1922 FILM *NOSFERATU: A SYMPHONY OF HORROR*)

Despite being a rip-off of the Dracula character, Count Orlok makes for a more frightening fiend thanks to freaky makeup effects and the chilling performance of German actor Max Schrek, who plays the titular nosferatu (a popular term for vampire). *SPECIAL POWER:* Without ever making a sound—*Nosferatu* is a silent film—Count Orlok instills a chill with evil glares and eerie gestures.

WELCOME TO
TRANSYLVANIA
A **TERRIFYING** TOUR

Cheesy Dracula-themed hotels and restaurants lure tourists to central Romania—the region historically known as Transylvania—yet much of the landscape remains unchanged since the days of Vlad the Impaler. Let's skulk past the tourist traps and explore the spookiest spots of Dracula's stalking grounds . . .

4. POENARI CASTLE

After his father and brother were assassinated, Vlad Dracula enslaved those responsible to rebuild this castle atop a windswept crag south of Transylvania. They worked until their clothes rotted away, then kept on working naked! When the castle came under assault of Turkish forces, Vlad's wife leaped to her death from a window rather than be taken prisoner. Today, Poenari Castle is a ruin reached by climbing 1,400 steps.

5. BORGO PASS

Although *Dracula* author Bram Stoker never visited Transylvania before he wrote his famous novel, he wisely chose this high mountain pass—aka Tihuta Pass—as the gateway to the Count's old country. Today, as in Stoker's novel, Borgo Pass leads to a countryside of rustic villages and rugged hills. Tourists will also find Dracula's Castle— a hotel complete with a crypt.

1. CARPATHIAN MOUNTAINS

The region of Transylvania is bordered to the east and south by this forbidding mountain range, home to such cheerily named geological features as "Hell Valley." Wander these mountains with caution. The forests are crawling with howling wolves and bears.

2. SIGHISOARA

If you're dead-set on visiting the birthplace of Count Dracula, this medieval city in the middle of Transylvania is the closest you'll get. Vlad Dracula—the bloodthirsty inspiration for Stoker's vampire—was born here in 1431. Dracula's address is 5 Cositorarilor Street, now home to a restaurant. A terror in his time, Vlad Dracula is a national hero today for his bravery in defending southern Romania from the Ottoman Empire.

6. SCHOLOMANCE

In Bram Stoker's novel, Count Dracula studies the dark arts at this magical academy run by the devil, based on a mythical school in the Transylvanian mountains. Was Scholomance a real place? We answer that question later in the chapter on witchcraft and wizardry.

3. RED LAKE

One of Transylvania's most popular getaways during the long days of the summer, remote Red Lake—also known as Killer Lake—takes on a creepy vibe once the crowds leave in autumn and the evening fog rolls across its red-tinged waters. According to legend, Red Lake is stained from the blood of shepherds crushed in an 1837 landslide.

AGENT JEEPER'S REALITY CHECK

Red Lake's bloody color has nothing to do with shepherds who may or may not have been crushed in a landslide more than a century ago. It's actually caused by a high concentration of ferric oxide, a chemical in the water.

NAME **CRP001**

Creepy Case File #1: Vampire Panic!

SUBJECT: The widespread practice of staking vampires in their graves

LOCATION: Europe, Russia, United States

TIME FRAME: A.D. 1500 to 2000

CASE BACKGROUND:

Thunk. The gravedigger's shovel hit something hard in the soggy soil of the village cemetery. Shoving the dark dirt aside, he revealed a crude wooden coffin to the villagers gathering at the graveside. They braced for the worst as the gravedigger manhandled the casket from the earth. After all, this was the coffin of Arnod Paole, an ex-soldier who complained of once tussling with a vampire. For a man who'd been dead and buried for 40 days—ever since breaking his neck in a wagon accident—Paole seemed to be leading a busy afterlife. Four people were already dead.

The gravedigger pried open the coffin. Inside, Paole's body lay in a pool of blood. His old skin and nails had slipped off, revealing a refreshed form. Blood oozed from Paole's nose, eyes, ears, and mouth, as if he'd risen recently for a messy midnight meal. Clutching their stakes, the villagers rushed in to exterminate the revenant.

This scene might sound right out of a horror film, but it really happened, around 1725, in the village of Medvegia in what is now Serbia. And it's far from an isolated incident. Many similar vampire panics drove frightened villagers and vampire hunters to dig up the corpses of suspected bloodsuckers—only to find their fangs running red and their bodies curiously free of decay. The exhumation of Arnod Paole ends with an especially gruesome twist. When the villagers drove a stake into his heart, the weeks-dead corpse let out a chilling moan.

WHY DID VILLAGERS **DIG UP CORPSES** TO **"KILL"** THEM A SECOND TIME?

The unearthing of vampire graves became such a rampant practice in the 1800s that officials began outlawing it. Nevertheless, it spread to the American colonies and continues to modern times. Six Roman men were arrested for illegally exhuming the body of a suspected *strigoi* in 2003.

CASE ANALYSIS:

Historians have no doubt that people throughout Europe, parts of Russia, and even the United States dug up (or exhumed) the bodies of suspected vampires only to kill them again by staking each corpse's heart, cutting off its head, or burning the remains—often doing all three! (You can never be too careful when disposing of a vampire.) Government officials and priests have documented such gruesome exhumations since the Middle Ages. Their reports are rife with descriptions of unearthed corpses sporting fresh skin, wide-open eyes, mouths trickling blood, and bloated bodies—allegedly from feeding on the living. Vampire panics were especially common during times of deadly plague. The disease's first victim typically took the blame as a vampire for the deaths of others. Rude exhumations and stakings followed.

But what vampire slayers considered surefire symptoms of an undead fiend are actually just part of the natural process of human decomposition. Weeks after death, a corpse's skin blisters, turns black, and begins slipping off, revealing a red-tinged body and nails that appear to have grown. Gas produced by bacteria in the gut inflates the body and forces putrid fluids from every opening, making the corpse look as if it recently feasted. That same gas could produce a sound from the mouth if squeezed from the chest—by impalement with a stake, for instance. In other words, Arnod Paole's final moan was nothing more than a post-burial burp.

ETHEL THE E.T.'S
DISTURBING DATA

Arnod Paole said he once banished a vampire by smearing himself with the creature's blood and eating dirt from its grave. What, did he run out of garlic?

Interview With a Real VAMPIRE

THEY MAY NOT BE THE VAMPIRES OF FICTION AND FOLKLORE, BUT THEY'VE INSPIRED PEOPLE AROUND THE WORLD TO EMBRACE THEIR BLOOD-SLURPING LIFESTYLE. Ethel the E.T. travels to New Orleans's French Quarter (in Louisiana, U.S.A.) to meet Belfazaar Ashantison, founder of the New Orleans Vampire Association. A "sanguine" vampire, Ashantison talks with Ethel about how he drinks blood to give him energy. But don't worry, he promises he won't bite—not without your permission, anyway.

Ethel: Should I be afraid of you?
Ashantison: I would suggest caution around anyone you are not familiar with. However, don't be afraid.

Ethel: Well, don't try anything funny—I'm packing garlic and holy water!
Ashantison: Garlic is great on spaghetti and buttered bread. Actually, garlic was used as a way to [cover up] the smell of decay during times of disease. Holy water, like any other water, will just make a vampire wet.

Ethel: Most vampires are made and not born. When and how did you "turn"?
Ashantison: The reality of the situation is that vampires are born this way. There was not a "turning" that came with it. "Turning" implies that it was either forcefully done to me or I had a choice to either become what I am or to move away from it.

Ethel: So do you really drink blood?
Ashantison: Yes, I do drink blood. However, I only drink blood from willing donors. It's not like we are out skulking in the shadows waiting to pounce on the unsuspecting.

Ethel: What does blood taste like?
Ashantison: It has a coppery tang to it that shifts a bit, becoming more coppery or less coppery depending on the diet and blood type of the donor. Sometimes it can be sweet. Sometimes it can be a bit on the salty side.

HE SIPS BLOOD AND AVOIDS THE SUN!
MEET A MODERN-DAY CREATURE OF THE NIGHT . . .

Ethel: **Drinking blood is dangerous—it can carry all kinds of diseases. Aren't you worried?**
Ashantison: Vampires who are smart get their donors and themselves tested on a regular basis. It is considered a great concern to both the vampire and donor and helps to alleviate any possibility of disease transmission.

Ethel: **What did your parents think when you came out of the coffin?**
Ashantison: They pretty much thought it was just a phase. I have been identifying myself as a vampire since the age of 13 and am now 48. My mom took it far better than my dad did—when they finally figured out this was not just some phase that I am going through. She actually went out of her way to try and understand [it], even to the point of accompanying me to a couple of doctors.

Ethel: **You must hang with a lot of real bloodsuckers. What do you all do for fun?**
Ashantison: The same things as anyone else. Personally, I go out with my friends and do everything from bowling to karaoke to fishing to whatever strikes our fancy. We are just like everyone else in the world.

Ethel: **You must be a night owl. Don't you miss the sun?**
Ashantison: I don't miss the sun at all . . . In reality, although many of the vampires in the community have a natural inclination toward the night, we get along pretty well in the day. It is because we are sensitive to energy around us that causes us discomfort during the daylight hours. After all, what is the sun? A bright ball of burning energy that circles the globe at regular intervals.

Ethel: **Do you sleep in a coffin?**
Ashantison: No, I actually sleep on a king-size bed. To be honest, I'm sort of claustrophobic, so having those walls around me would make me feel as though things were closing in on me.

Ethel: **Vampires are scary for most people. As a vampire, what scares you?**
Ashantison: Politicians.

Ethel: **What's the one myth you'd like to dispel about modern vampires?**
Ashantison: We are not some sort of supernatural force to be reckoned with. We are, in fact, just like everyone else around you. We work, raise our children, pay our bills . . . We are your neighbors, uncles, aunts, mothers, sisters, brothers, fathers, and cousins . . . We are that point where fantasy and reality collide into being. For beings that "feed" off of other people, many of us tend to work in healing careers.

AGENT JEEPER'S REALITY CHECK
I don't know, Ethel—vampires only exist in books and movies. Anything beyond that is just performance art.

CREEPY EQUIPMENT
VAMPIRE-KILLING KIT

VITAL VIALS These glass bottles contain essential undead deterrents: holy water, sacred oil, and garlic. The water and oil burned vampires on contact. Stinky garlic, recognized since ancient times as a remedy and immunity booster, warded against bloodsuckers—probably why you never hear of a vampire ordering out for Italian.

LIGHT READING A Book of Common Prayer, dated from 1857, contains empowering passages to embolden tourists in the old country.

CROSSING GUARDS Unclean creatures, vampires feared the sacred might of crucifixes and rosary beads. Just the sight of them sent bloodsuckers scurrying into the shadows.

VAMPIRES WERE ONCE CONSIDERED A REAL PAIN IN THE NECK FOR TRAVELERS IN EASTERN EUROPE. Smart tourists packed protection—a wooden case loaded with everything that bloodsuckers loathe. So goes the legend of the "vampire-killing kit."

More than 80 of these sturdy, road-ready caskets have been identified, according to Jonathan Ferguson, curator of firearms at the Royal Armouries Museum in England. Although the kits look ancient and contain antique instruments, Ferguson suspects they were assembled in the 20th century as creepy novelties to cash in on the Dracula craze. Here's a painstaking guide to the sharp objects, sacred substances, and other vampire-stopping goodies found inside one such kit, a mahogany casket on display at the Royal Armouries Museum ...

ENCOURAGING WORDS A scrap in the kit's lid offers this handwritten snippet of scripture: "But those mine enemies, which would not that I should reign over them, bring hither, and slay them before me."

RAISING THE STAKES The kit's ultimate weapons, the hammer and wooden stakes would put a permanent end to any blood-sucker caught napping in a coffin. The kit also contains a pistol and tool for making silver bullets, a more modern means of vanquishing vampires.

VAMPIRE AT LARGE!

Fear of the undead is alive and well in one Serbian village.

Villagers string garlic across their windows and keep crosses within easy reach in Zarozje, a remote town surrounded by a dense oak forest in Serbia. Word is out: A vampire is on the loose! In 2012, the village council warned of an ancient bloodsucking creature named Sava Savanovic prowling around town, possibly looking for a midnight snack. Residents stocked up on stakes.

Serbia and vampires go way back. Remember Arnod Paole and Peter Plogojowitz from earlier in this chapter? Both suspected blood-guzzlers hailed from this region. The term "vampire" spawned from a Serbian word, and fear of these creatures never quite died in rural parts of the nation. It's no surprise, then, that Zarozje's residents took their council's warning to heart—especially because they knew the legend of Sava Savanovic.

The rickety wooden mill by the river just outside Zarozje might not look like the sort of place any self-respecting vampire would call home, but that's where Savanovic was said to dwell. According to lore, he pounced on villagers foolish enough to grind their grain at the mill. But when Savanovic's riverside shack collapsed in early 2012, residents feared he would wander the countryside until he found a new home. That's when the council issued its warning, and villagers began eyeing the fog at twilight for suspicious shapes.

Some locals think the Savanovic scare is just a story to boost tourism in this poverty-stricken part of the world. Sightseers who visit the mill can decide for themselves. Was that whispery rustle just the wind in the trees, or is Sava Savanovic lurking in the mists?

VAMPIRES UNEARTHED!

Meanwhile, in the neighboring nation of Bulgaria, archaeologists dug up a 700-year-old skeleton that had taken a serious beating. Its teeth were missing. Someone had thrust an iron rod through its chest. The researchers recognized these telltale injuries from a hundred other ancient graves unearthed across the nation. These were the bodies of suspected vampires, defanged and staked to the ground in the Middle Ages to ensure they would never rise to prey on the living.

THE VAMPIRE BAT

O nce twilight descends on parts of Central and South America, a creepy creature of the night stretches its leathery wings and takes flight. It's on the hunt for a dozing animal; any pig, chicken, horse, or cow will do. Named the vampire bat after the night-prowling monsters of legend, this furry winged mammal has the body of a mouse and the appetite of a competitive eater. Tonight, like every other night, it hungers for blood.

Once the bat spies a snoozing victim, it lands silently nearby and creeps like a spider on legs and arms adapted for crawling. Using heat sensors in its nose, the bat scans its prey's body for spots where blood flows just beneath the skin. Then, almost gently ... *snikt!* Razor-sharp fangs open the tiniest cut in the dozing victim's body. Warm blood begins to ooze.

Lick, lick, lick. With a grooved tongue made for lapping, the agile bat can slurp blood for more than 30 minutes without waking its host. Between sunset and sunrise, a typical vampire bat will consume half its weight in blood. That's the same as you gulping six gallons (23 liters) of the red stuff in one night!

The bat's victims usually awaken unharmed and unaware that they've been bitten, although the bites can spread a deadly disease called rabies. Farm animals have the most to fear from these twilight terrors. People can sleep more easily—bat bites on humans are unheard of.

Well, almost. Sweet dreams!

blood

Bram Stoker's Count Dracula was the original Batman. He enjoyed night flights as a winged rodent—although it was too large to be a vampire bat.

ETHEL THE E.T.'S
DISTURBING DATA

Vampire bats have an anticlotting substance in their spit to keep their victim's blood flowing smoothly for the feast. The substance's name: Draculin.

BLOODY BEASTS

SHARP-BEAKED GROUND FINCH: It might not look nearly as sinister as the vampire bat, but this bold bird of the Galápagos Islands becomes just as bloodthirsty. During the sweltering dry season, it pecks beneath the feathers of larger seabirds to rip open oozing wounds for a refreshing drink of hot blood.

VAMPIRE MOTH: This close relative of fruit-slurping moth species has developed a disturbing diet. It drills its barb-lined tongue into human skin and then slowly drinks its fill.

REGAL HORNED LIZARD: While all the other creatures here drink blood for dinner, this thick-skinned lizard pumps plasma to avoid becoming dinner. The regal horned lizard can squirt a stream of sticky blood from its tear ducts to frighten away predators. Animals 20 times its size fear this lizard's bloodshot eyes!

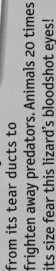

Vampires

AIIIIEEEE!	Count Orlok
TERRIFYING	Peter Plogojowitz
SPINE-TINGLING	Count Dracula
	Belfazaar Ashantison
UNSETTLING	Lilith
	Vampire Bat

PhEAR FACTOR

PHENOMENA ELICITING ABNORMAL REACTIONS

Agent Jeeper Ranks **BLOODSUCKING FIENDS.**

31

CHAPTER 2

Horrible
Brutes

IF VAMPIRES ARE THE SOPHISTICATED ARISTOCRATS OF THE MONSTER WORLD, THEN GET READY TO MEET THE CRUDE CASTOFFS OF THEIR SCARY SOCIETY.

Possessed of superhuman strength and insatiable hunger, the shaggy beasts and shambling horrors in this chapter chew more than just the scenery in horror movies. Prepare to learn the terrifying truth behind zombies, werewolves, and … worse. Don't bother trying to reason with these creatures. If you see one, run!

CHANGE IS BAD

THE LEGEND OF LYCANTHROPY

AHHHH-WOOOOH! FEW SOUNDS CHILL THE BLOOD LIKE THE HOWL OF A WOLF, PARTICULARLY WHEN IT ECHOES THROUGH A FOREST LIT BY THE FULL MOON. Never mind that people have little to fear from wild wolves, which rarely attack humans. The howl brings to mind a supernatural stalker famous for its fur, fangs, and fury—the werewolf.

Unlike full-time terrors such as demons and zombies, werewolves lead double lives: ordinary humans by day and shaggy monsters by night. They suffer from lycanthropy (from the Greek words for "wolf" and "human"), a condition that triggers a change for the worse. Werewolves in monster mode sprout hair everywhere and shed their humanity, becoming mindless beasts that maul anyone in sight. Former friends become wolf chow.

You might think it takes a chomp from another werewolf and a full moon to unleash a lycanthrope's inner beast, but those are only recent additions to their legend (along with the use of silver bullets to deliver the killing blow). European folklore offers many triggers for transformation, including curses from the gods, magic creams, wolf-pelt belts, or pacts with the devil. Some people simply chose to become lycanthropes, but the only permanent cure was death. Well, usually. Vanquished werewolves occasionally rose from their graves—as vampires!

FAMOUS FURBALLS

THE GOOD: REMUS LUPIN (FROM THE HARRY POTTER SERIES)

Although this professor teaches defenses against the dark arts at the Hogwarts School of Witchcraft and Wizardry, he is harboring a grim secret—he is actually a werewolf! Despite his wild side, Remus is a vital ally for Harry Potter in his battle against the evil Voldemort.

THE BAD: LARRY TALBOT (FROM THE 1941 FILM *THE WOLF MAN*)

This film and its sequels establish nearly every modern werewolf rule. Talbot catches a mean case of lycanthropy after surviving a werewolf attack. The flowering of a poisonous plant called wolfsbane triggers his change, although in later films it's the light of the full moon.

THE STUDLY: JACOB BLACK (FROM THE TWILIGHT SERIES)

This Native American werewolf competes for the affections of Bella Swan, a human girl pining for the teenage vampire Edward Cullen. Ultimately, Swan ends up swooning for both of these strapping supernatural creatures.

ETHEL THE E.T.'S DISTURBING DATA

One of the first famous werewolves was King Lycaon, who was turned into a wolf after serving human flesh to Zeus. I guess the lesson here is never tick off the top god of Greek mythology!

Werewolves on Trial

ALONG WITH WITCHES AND VAMPIRES, WEREWOLVES WERE CONSIDERED PUBLIC ENEMIES in Europe—and particularly France—in the 16th and 17th centuries. Thousands of alleged lycanthropes were arrested and put on trial. Here are three of the creepiest cases...

GILLES GARNIER (FRANCE, 1573)
ALIAS: THE WEREWOLF OF DOLE

CASE BACKGROUND: When the bodies of several children turned up partially eaten near the town of Dole, authorities suspected they had a werewolf on the loose and encouraged the public to hunt the beast down. One night, some villagers stumbled across a local hermit named Gilles Garnier stooped over the body of a child. In the dim moonlight, he looked like a wolf! Certain they had found their man-beast, the villagers grabbed Garnier and hauled him away for trial.

CONFESSION: Garnier claimed he had made a pact with a forest spirit in exchange for a magical goop that shifted his shape. Once smeared with the substance, he allegedly became a wolf with a mad appetite for peopleburger.

SENTENCE: The Werewolf of Dole was burned alive at the stake.

PETER STUMPF (GERMANY, 1590)
ALIAS: THE WEREWOLF OF BEDBURG

CASE BACKGROUND: Perhaps the most famous—and sensationalized—of the many werewolf trials was that of Peter Stumpf, a farmer reportedly captured while in his furry werewolf form. He was charged with a long list of horrific crimes, including the killing and eating of women, children, and cattle.

CONFESSION: Under threat of torture, Stumpf confessed that the devil made him do it, granting him a belt that triggered his transformation into a bloodthirsty wolf. Mysteriously, the diabolical belt vanished after Stumpf's confession. The German authorities assumed the devil snatched it back.

SENTENCE: Stumpf was tortured to death in ways much too gruesome to recount.

JEAN GRENIER (FRANCE, 1603)
ALIAS: THE WEREWOLF OF LANDES

CASE BACKGROUND: Nearly 400 years before the movie *Teen Wolf*, a 13-year-old French boy named Jean Grenier claimed that he routinely transformed into a beast to kill dogs, eat children, and stalk pretty girls. Admitting that lycanthropy ran in the family, Grenier claimed his dad was also a werewolf.

CONFESSION: Far from being ashamed, Grenier boasted of his beastly abilities and grisly exploits. He said he could change into a wolf whenever he wished by applying a lotion and donning wolf furs—gifts from a shadowy forest lord.

SENTENCE: Declared insane, Grenier was sent to live in a monastery. His dad was cleared of werewolf charges.

AGENT JEEPER'S
REALITY CHECK

What do you think is more likely: That the accused criminals in these trials were actual werewolves, or that they were delusional troublemakers who blamed their behavior on lycanthropy? The threat of torture no doubt motivated some of these convicted "werewolves" to admit their shape-changing ways, as well.

THE BEAST OF

THE BEAST CROUCHED IN THE FOREST, SNIFFING AT THE COWS GRAZING NEARBY. THEY DIDN'T INTEREST HER. INSTEAD, SHE LOCKED HER SENSES ON THE GROUP OF CHILDREN GUARDING THE LIVESTOCK. THE BEAST CREPT CLOSER, CAREFUL TO STAY DOWNWIND SO THE CHILDREN WOULDN'T DETECT HER HORRID STENCH. SINGLING OUT THE YOUNGEST—AN EIGHT-YEAR-OLD BOY—SHE POUNCED.

The landscape of southern France looked straight out of a fairy tale in the 1700s, dotted with medieval hamlets and covered in hilly forests. Across this fantasy landscape prowled a very real monster. The attacks began in summer 1764, when the beast devoured a 14-year-old girl. More killings quickly followed, four in September alone. Soon, everyone in southern France—peasants and nobles alike—lived in terror of the "beast of Gévaudan," named for the region where she originally lurked.

GÉVAUDAN

When the beast of Gévaudan began prowling the French countryside in 1764, many villagers cried "loup-garou": "werewolf!"

Survivors described a wolflike creature, usually female, as large as a donkey, with reddish fur and a black stripe down her back like a hyena. She moved at supernatural speeds and could swing her tail like a whip. In some accounts, the beast walked upright on her hind legs. Many peasants believed she was a loup-garou: French for "werewolf."

Hunters swore that bullets, knives, and spears bounced off her foul-smelling hide. But the beast of Gévaudan met her match in early 1765, when she set upon a group of seven children tending cattle. *CONTINUED ON THE NEXT PAGE.*

This statue shows one tough 12-year-old, Jacques Portefaix, leading his friends in driving off the beast. France's King Louis XV rewarded him with gold and an education.

The beast leaped into the children's midst, snatching the youngest in her jaws. Expecting the others to flee in terror, she bounded away with her prey—but she didn't get very far. The oldest of the children, 12-year-old Jacques Portefaix, led the group in a daring counterattack.

Wielding knives and sticks, they chased the beast into a bog until she became stuck in the muck. Portefaix and his pals stabbed and walloped the snarling beast until she finally released her prey and wriggled free to flee into the forest. The victim survived, and the brave young Portefaix became a national hero. The King of France granted him rich rewards.

Unfortunately, after licking her wounds, the beast of Gévaudan resumed skulking about the French countryside. Even groups of heavily armed travelers weren't safe. The death toll rose to 60—as high as a hundred by some accounts. In June 1765, she stalked and killed four people in just one week.

ETHEL THE E.T.'S

DISTURBING DATA

Lycanthropic legends aren't confined to Europe. Tales of the loup-garou spread through French-speaking regions of Canada. Wisconsin is home to the "Beast of Bray Road," a wolfish creature first reported in the 1980s.

The King declared war on the beast, placing a large bounty on her hide. Hunters and soldiers scoured the fields and forests. One of the royal huntsmen brought down a massive gray wolf in September 1765. The carcass was stuffed and displayed at the Royal Palace of Versailles as the famous beast of Gévaudan, yet the attacks continued.

In the summer of 1767, a crack-shot hunter named Jean Chastel encountered another large creature and shot it with his rifle. According to a later account, he used a silver bullet. The beast of Gévaudan never killed again.

To this day, the species of the beast remains unknown. Historians suspect it was actually several animals, likely rabid wolves or perhaps a dog-wolf hybrid. "It certainly wasn't a hyena—not in Europe," says wolf researcher Dr. Rolf Peterson. "And it wasn't a werewolf. Not on this planet."

HAIR EVERYWHERE

IT WASN'T THE FULL MOON OR A MAGIC OINTMENT THAT TURNED PETRUS GONZALES INTO A WOLFMAN IN THE 16TH CENTURY. He was born that way. Gonzales suffered from hypertrichosis, also known as "werewolf syndrome." It's a rare genetic disorder that causes hair to grow everywhere it's not supposed to on the chest and face—even on the eyelids. (And you thought your dad was hairy!) Fewer than 50 people with hypertrichosis have been identified since Gonzales—the first known case—was born in 1551.

You would think that life for this furry fellow would have been, well, hairy! After all, werewolves were considered a real-life danger in the 16th century. Instead of being labeled a monster and driven from society, however, Gonzales became a sensation. After he was discovered as a boy on the Canary Islands, Gonzales was taken to France and raised at the palace of King Henry II. He received an education, learning courtly manners and Latin, the language of the well-to-do. Smart and sharply dressed in royal finery, Gonzales became the talk of Paris. He married and had children, who were born with the same hair-raising condition. The family toured Europe as celebrities. Nobles and princes treated them like royalty.

AGENT JEEPER'S REALITY CHECK

I can think of more likely sources of the werewolf myth, such as medieval outlaws and poachers living wild in the forests. And then we have the fearsome Norse warriors called "berserkers" who wore wolf pelts before going into battle. If you saw an army of snarling shaggy men charging in your direction, you'd believe in werewolves, too!

Today, people born with werewolf syndrome still get the star treatment. Consider Jesus "Chuy" Aceves, a circus performer who's traveled the world and appeared on television to showcase his hairy face. Like a modern-day Petrus Gonzales, Aceves is a sensation wherever he goes, and his condition comes with one other perk. "Women like hairy men," Aceves explained in an interview, "and I get a lot of proposals."

Jesus "Chuy" Aceves comes from the world's hairiest family. Nineteen of his relatives have hypertrichosis.

Walking

Stiffs

MUMMiES! DOOM FROM THE TOMB

It's a creepy scenario played out in countless scary movies and horror novels (including one by *Dracula* author Bram Stoker): Archaeologists exploring a dusty Egyptian burial site unwittingly trigger a curse that disturbs its lone inhabitant, a mummified corpse. The bandaged body stirs, opening its dark eyes and uncrossing its arms. Shaking off cobwebs, the mummy emerges from its sarcophagus to plod among the pyramids, using superhuman strength to crush the life from the living and restore its pre-preserved form. You can hardly blame the mummy for being in a bad mood. How would you feel if someone woke you from a 3,000-year dirt nap?

THE ROTTEN TRUTH: Although many cultures left a legacy of preserved dead, Hollywood's mummies always hail from ancient Egypt. The Egyptians believed the spirits of their dearly departed would wither without access to their former bodies, so priests perfected the process of mummification to keep corpses from rotting away. They removed all the organs except the heart, then packed the body cavity with an Egyptian salt called natron that soaked up moisture. Considered useless, the brain was yanked through the nose with an iron hook. So remember, the next time you see a mummy in a horror movie, it's brainless!

FROM THESE SHAMBLING DEAD!

ZOMBiES! HUNGRY HUMAN HERD

Hollywood's most hideous monsters, zombies are walking corpses, half decayed and smelling like death warmed over. Driven by their appetite for human flesh (and a heaping side of brains), they stumble along with their arms outstretched, clawing after the living, never tiring. If one of these walking dead sinks its teeth into your tender skin, you'll become a zombie, too. More than just foul, zombies are infectious!

THE ROTTEN TRUTH: The closest thing to a zombie in European folklore is the dreaded revenant, seen shambling from the grave in chapter one. African and Haitian history, on the other hand, is filled with references to the Z-word. Practitioners of voodoo—a religion that originated in West Africa—believe that sorcerers known as "bokors" can combine spells and "zombie powder" to resurrect the recently deceased and turn them into mindless slaves. The key ingredients of the powder are charred bones, bits of toad, exotic plants, and pufferfish—which contain neurotoxins that can cause paralysis and death. Victims of zombification allegedly keel over, then recover in a vegetative state and ready to follow orders. The zombie is hidden away from friends and sentenced to hard labor, a fate worse than death.

AGENT JEEPER'S REALITY CHECK

The only "walking dead" I'm aware of were unfortunate folks accidentally buried alive in the days before doctors could diagnose death with 100 percent accuracy. Fears of such a claustrophobic fate—imagine being buried alive in a casket!—fed the success of "life-revival devices" such as the Bateson's Belfry. Invented in 1852, it was a coffin-mounted bell that panicked people could ring if they woke up six feet under!

INTERNATIONAL
NIGHTMARES

GHOUL

WHERE DOES IT LIVE? Middle East

WHAT IS IT? The good news is this undead demon doesn't prey on the living. The bad news? It munches on the disgusting dead. Giving a morbid meaning to the phrase "dig in," ghouls lurk in graveyards and unearth bodies to devour their rotting guts.

FREAKIEST FACT: Shape-changing ghouls can take the appearance of the last corpse they chomped. They literally are what they eat!

AHUIZOTL

WHERE DOES IT LIVE? Aquatic caves in Mexico

WHAT IS IT? A sleek water beast similar to a river otter, the ahuizotl isn't so horrible except for one disturbing detail: Its tail is topped with a human hand! The creature uses this extra extremity to grab unsuspecting swimmers and drown them in the dark depths.

FREAKIEST FACT: According to Aztec legend, ahuizotl victims bob to the surface without eyes, teeth, or fingernails!

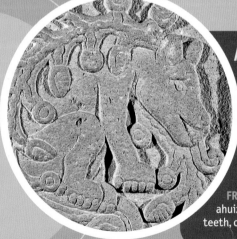

LOATHSOME
LEGENDS
FROM AROUND
THE WORLD

RAKSHASA

WHERE DOES IT LIVE?
India and Southeast Asia

WHAT IS IT? This hulking demon from Hindu mythology poisons its victims with its toxic claws before chowing down with saber-sharp fangs. Said to have bottomless bellies, rakshasas are always on the prowl for fresh flesh.

FREAKIEST FACT:
Rakshasas are sorcerers as well as cannibals, able to alter their size and appearance. They can take the form of any animal or person—even your math teacher!

BUNYIP

WHERE DOES IT LIVE? Swamps and creeks of Australia

WHAT IS IT? Australia's most feared river critter isn't the crocodile. The continent's original residents recount tales of a seal-like water spirit that lunges from water holes to snatch unwary bathers in its tusks.

FREAKIEST FACT: An Australian museum displayed a supposed bunyip skull in the 1840s (although experts claimed the bone was from a baby cow with birth defects).

ANKOU

WHERE DOES IT LIVE? Ancient cemeteries in France

WHAT IS IT? Riding atop a coach drawn by charging black stallions, this cloaked figure collects the souls of doomed people. (So if you see him pulling into your driveway, pretend you're not home!) When he's not on the road, the ankou skulks through moonlit cemeteries like a security guard for the dead.

FREAKIEST FACT: The ankou's true form is revealed each time a gust of wind lifts his ragged hood. He's a living skeleton!

MANIMALS!

FAMILIAR FISH: Meet the world's ugliest mermaids! Two female carp raised in a private South Korean pond made the news for their freakishly humanlike faces. Bred as hybrids of two carp species, both fish have slender lips, forward-facing eyes, and long noses—faces that only their proud owner could love.

CREEPY CHOPPERS: The sheepshead looks like your typical ocean fish until you ask it to say "ahhh." Its opened mouth reveals a set of pearly whites that look just like human teeth! The fish evolved this winning smile to chomp on crabs and oysters, its favorite foods.

MORBID MOTH: As if the skull-like pattern on its back—from which it gets its common name—wasn't scary enough, the death's-head moth makes a creepy squeaking noise when it's in a bad mood. Although not dangerous to people, the moth appears in many scary stories and tales of the supernatural.

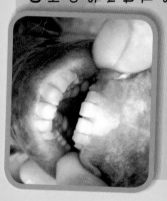

Mindless MONSTERS

PHENOMENA ELICITING ABNORMAL REACTIONS

PhEAR FACTOR

Ethel the E.T. Ranks **HORRIBLE BRUTES.**

AIIIIEEEE!

Beast of Gévaudan

Ghouls

TERRIFYING

Werewolves

SPINE-TINGLING

Zombies

Rakshasas

UNSETTLING

Mummies

49

CHAPTER 3

Cryptic Creatures

A FURRY BLUR IN THE FOREST. MYSTERIOUS WAKES IN A SCOTTISH LAKE. FREAKY BEASTS THAT WASH UP ON THE BEACH. When Mother Nature gets creepy, creature hunters come running. These "cryptozoologists" scour the wilderness and dive beneath the waves for proof that some monsters are more than mythical. Turn the page to join the hunt for Bigfoot, the Loch Ness Monster, and other "cryptids"—animals that exist only in legend. Oh, and don't forget your camera. You never know when you might encounter a shipwrecking Kraken … or a "goat-sucking" Chupacabra!

BIGFOOT FORWARD

THE SEARCH FOR SASQUATCH

FALL 2011: Two campers in the Cascades found themselves face-to-waist with a furry 9-foot (2.7-m)-tall creature, its yellow eyes glaring in their flashlight beam. Winter 1979: A passenger riding on a remote northern California, U.S.A., highway peered out his window to see a muscular beast covered in darkish hair crossing a creekbed. Summer 1924: Gold prospectors in the Washington, U.S.A., woods awakened to the thunderous racket of "mountain gorillas" pounding on their cabin's walls.

This book doesn't have enough pages to detail every eyewitness account—more than 3,000 in all—of the apelike creature said to wander the wilderness of the Pacific Northwest and elsewhere. You know the hairy giant as Bigfoot, aka Sasquatch (a term based on a Native American name for the many wild men of North American folklore). Sasquatch sightings go back centuries, and today the beast is a central figure in cryptozoology. But is Bigfoot real? That's the million-dollar question.

No, seriously! A binocular company offered a million bucks in 2008 to anyone who could prove Bigfoot's existence! The cash went unclaimed. And despite decades of Bigfoot hunting, no one has recovered a body of the beast—a fact often cited by skeptics as proof that Bigfoot is bogus. Yet true believers claim that evidence abounds. They point to samples of supposed Sasquatch fur that don't match any known animal. They replay famous 1967 film footage of a female apelike creature striding through the northern California wilderness while peering creepily over her shoulder at cameramen. And they follow the footprints—perhaps the most compelling evidence of all. Turn the page to find out why.

SASQUATCH Suspects
BEASTS THAT FIT THE BIGFOOT BILL

GIGANTOPITHECUS
This oversize ape went extinct 100,000 years ago. Could a small population have survived?

NEANDERTHALS
Some cryptozoologists suspect that Sasquatch represents a "missing link" between humans and their hairy ancestors.

ANOTHER "GREAT APE"
Bigfoot could be an undiscovered member of the family that includes chimpanzees, gorillas, orangutans, and humans.

INTERDIMENSIONAL MONSTERS
Native Americans believed in a wide variety of "wild men" with magical powers.

BEARS
Skeptics think eyewitnesses are confusing bears for Bigfoot.

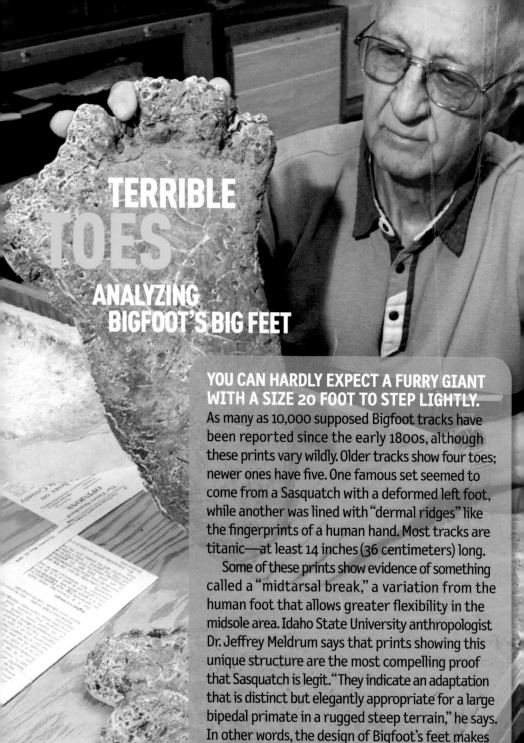

TERRIBLE TOES

ANALYZING BIGFOOT'S BIG FEET

YOU CAN HARDLY EXPECT A FURRY GIANT WITH A SIZE 20 FOOT TO STEP LIGHTLY. As many as 10,000 supposed Bigfoot tracks have been reported since the early 1800s, although these prints vary wildly. Older tracks show four toes; newer ones have five. One famous set seemed to come from a Sasquatch with a deformed left foot, while another was lined with "dermal ridges" like the fingerprints of a human hand. Most tracks are titanic—at least 14 inches (36 centimeters) long.

Some of these prints show evidence of something called a "midtarsal break," a variation from the human foot that allows greater flexibility in the midsole area. Idaho State University anthropologist Dr. Jeffrey Meldrum says that prints showing this unique structure are the most compelling proof that Sasquatch is legit. "They indicate an adaptation that is distinct but elegantly appropriate for a large bipedal primate in a rugged steep terrain," he says. In other words, the design of Bigfoot's feet makes scientific sense for a creature that's most at home in a hilly wilderness.

A HAIRY DEBATE

AGENT JEEPER AND ETHEL THE E.T. BUTT HEADS OVER BIGFOOT . . .

AGENT JEEPER	ETHEL THE E.T.

Topic 1: Bodies of Evidence

Only a crackpot would think Sasquatch is legit. Surely a hunter or hiker would've come across a dead one by now.	Um, hello? Bigfoot shares the woods with all kinds of scavenging animals, remember? All those critters make quick work of bones and bodies. Anything left breaks down quickly in the acidic soils.

Topic 2: Making Tracks

I suppose you put a lot of faith in the footprints, then. Hate to break it to you, but a prankster named Raymond Wallace created some of the most famous Sasquatch tracks in the 1950s while stomping around northern California in oversize wooden feet.	Sure, Wallace and his family fooled a lot of people with their phony tracks, but what about the thousands of footprints discovered elsewhere? They can't all be fake!

Topic 3: Monkey Business

Hollywood special effects experts think the female Bigfoot in that 1967 footage was just a guy in a gorilla suit. Two people have even taken the credit for wearing the costume.	That film is kinda fishy, I'll give you that, but those claims haven't been proven. And some experts insist that a man in a suit wouldn't match the dimensions and movements of the creature in the footage.

Topic 4: Nowhere to Hide

Bigfoot believers estimate that up to 6,000 of the hairy hominids exist in the wild. Wouldn't we have seen one by now? I mean, humans are everywhere!	Oh, pffft! Tell that to the scientists who found 125,000 previously uncounted lowland gorillas in Central Africa in 2008. Or to the explorer who discovered the mythical zebra-donkey-giraffe mash-up known as the okapi in 1901. The wilderness is still big enough for Bigfoot to hide!

THE TWIN BROTHER: YETI

WHERE DOES IT LURK? The Himalaya

Bigfoot's cold-weather equivalent, the Yeti (pronounced "yet-ee"), is said to roam the icy wastes of the world's tallest peaks. Sir Edmund Hillary—one of the first men to climb Mount Everest—claimed he spotted supersize footprints during his climb (although he later became a Yeti skeptic). Despite depictions of a white-furred monster, most eyewitnesses describe a creature identical to Bigfoot, except shaggier.

WHAT SETS IT APART? Although "the abominable snowman" has a reputation for fierceness (Himalayans claim it kills yaks with one punch), French explorer Captain d'Auvergne swore the Yeti had a sweet side. After losing his way in the snow in 1938, d'Auvergne said the beast fed and cared for him in a cave, nursing him back to health.

AGENT JEEPER'S REALITY CHECK

Scientists suspect that the Yeti is actually a Tibetan brown bear. Analysis of Zana's genetic material, meanwhile, revealed that she was a regular human rather than a refugee from some long-lost Neanderthal tribe (see p. 57).

Bigfoot
Family
Reunion

We track down Sasquatch's distant relatives . . .

THE MONKEYLIKE UNCLE: YOWIE

WHERE DOES IT LURK? Rain forests throughout Australia
Australia's original inhabitants told campfire tales of this "great hairy man," a sacred creature thought to prowl the forests since the creation of the world. Known by many names—including the "Yahoo"—the Yowie is said to move through the darkest reaches of the rain forest like a spindly limbed gorilla, glaring at bush travelers with blazing eyes set beneath a broad forehead.

WHAT SETS IT APART? Perhaps the most aggressive of the hairy giants, the Yowie has been blamed for stealing livestock, chasing children—even killing a puppy!

THE LITTLE SISTER: ZANA THE ALMA

WHERE DOES IT LURK? Mountainous regions of Central Asia
For centuries, villagers in this part of the world have reported sightings of so-called Almas—primitive shaggy people that look more like Neanderthal cave dwellers than apelike beasts. The most famous Alma of all was Zana, a wild mountain woman caught in a Russian village in 1850.

WHAT SETS IT APART? At first aggressive and unable to talk, Zana eventually settled into village life. She even had children with one of the villagers.

THE BLACK SHEEP OF THE FAMILY: SKUNK APE

WHERE DOES IT LURK? Florida's Everglades
Meet Bigfoot's smellier cousin from America's steamy south. Eyewitnesses describe the skunk ape as a 7-foot (2.1-m) monster with reddish fur, sort of like an oversize orangutan.

WHAT SETS IT APART? True to its name, the skunk ape gives off a deathly aroma, one that witnesses claim they smell long before they spot the creature. It's described as a mix of rotten eggs, cow poop, and a wet dog that's never gotten a bath.

Creepy Case File #2: Corpse of the Goat Sucker

SUBJECT: The Chupacabra, a blood-guzzling cryptid

LOCATION: Puerto Rico, Brazil, Mexico, and the southwestern United States

TIME FRAME: A.D. 1995 to 2010

CASE BACKGROUND:

Just the mention of its name sends farmers scrambling to lock up their livestock. The Chupacabra, Spanish for "goat sucker," reportedly began prowling the island of Puerto Rico in the mid-1990s. Early eyewitness accounts described a creature more like a space alien than an Earth animal. Four feet (1.2 m) long from head to tail, it had leathery skin, eyes that shone like headlights, and a back lined with spines. It hopped like a kangaroo and hissed when startled. Some witnesses even claimed it could fly. According to sightings, the Chupacabra crept into barnyard pens in the dead of night and sucked the blood from frightened chickens, cows, and goats—hence its nasty nickname.

Theories for the Chupacabra's origin abound. Some believe it's the runaway pet of an alien who dropped by Earth for a pit stop. Others insist it's an escapee from some mad scientist's lab. The creature's resemblance to a monster in the 1995 movie *Species* led to speculation that the "goat sucker" might just be imaginary or—worse—a hoax.

DID SCIENTISTS RECOVER THE MANGY REMAINS OF THIS BARNYARD TERROR?

CASE ANALYSIS:

As Chupacabra sightings spread to other parts of the world, eyewitness descriptions began to change. Farmers in Mexico and the southwestern United States reported seeing hairless doglike monsters attacking their livestock. A Texas sheriff's deputy recorded video of a long-snouted beast padding down a dusty back road. Panicked ranchers began shooting the creatures, giving researchers an opportunity they never had with Bigfoot and other cryptids. Suddenly, scientists could study Chupacabras in the flesh!

Analysis revealed that these goat suckers weren't really alien monsters or coyotes. They were coyotes suffering from scabies, a painful skin experiments gone awry. Too weakened condition that leaves the poor animals looking mangy and monstrous. Too weakened by the disease to stalk normal prey, the stricken coyotes attacked easier-to-kill barnyard animals, spreading the Chupacabra legend in the process. But while scientists have identified the hairless monster prowling the Mexico border, the original goat sucker of Puerto Rico—the glaring, spine-backed beast—remains a mystery.

LURKER IN THE LAKE

What's making waves in the murky waters of Loch Ness?

Rolling hills, foggy forests, and even a medieval castle fill the fairy-tale landscape around Loch Ness, Scotland's second largest lake, but travelers trek here for more than just the breathtaking scenery. Eyeing every suspicious ripple, alert for any weird wake, they scan the dark waters for a glimpse of the world's most famous aquatic oddity: the Loch Ness Monster. You might know her as "Nessie."

Although Bigfoot reigns as the king of the cryptids on land, Nessie rules the watery realm. Depictions of a serpentine beast date back 2,000 years—back to when a fearsome tattooed tribe known as the Picts chiseled the image of a finned creature onto large stones near the lake. Five centuries later, according to one written account, an Irish monk invoked the power of prayer to repel a monster poised to gobble a Loch Ness bather.

A series of high-profile sightings in the 1930s transformed Nessie from a creature of folklore into a cryptozoolgy superstar. More than 4,000 eyewitness accounts of a massive lake monster—some verified by lie-detector testing—have been reported since. As with

Sasquatch, many of these sightings and photographs were proven as hoaxes (see page 147 for the most famous example), but that hasn't dampened the enthusiasm of true Nessie believers. Their number one Nessie suspect: the plesiosaur, a long-necked marine dinosaur that was supposed to have died out with *T-rex* and his kin 65 million years ago. Could a small population of these titanic terrors have survived to swim upstream into Loch Ness?

Nessie skeptics believe the sightings are simply cases of mistaken identity. After all, European otters, dogpaddling deer, and large sturgeon fish can look mysterious when their backs break the surface of the lake. High-tech sonar searches have turned up nothing conclusive from the lake's murky depths. And yet the search for Nessie continues. At least one website maintains a live camera view of the lake, encouraging viewers to keep a round-the-clock vigil for suspicious activity. The ancient Picts may have recorded Nessie in stone; modern creature hunters can now tag the beast online.

More Lake Monstrosities!

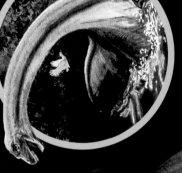

ETHEL THE E.T.'S DISTURBING DATA

A British marathon runner spent 12 days running along the bottom of Loch Ness in an antique diving outfit for charity. He never had a run-in with Nessie—although he did trip and hurt his shoulder in the zero-visibility murk.

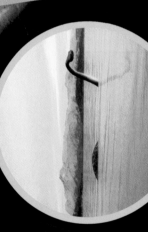

CHAMP The chilly waters of New England's Lake Champlain are supposedly home to this Nessie-style plesiosaur.

OGOPOGO This sea serpent with a funny name is said to lurk in Okanagan Lake in British Columbia, Canada.

61

QUEST FOR THE KRAKEN

We go fishing for a mariner's nightmare

THE CREATURE ROSE FROM THE INKY DARKNESS OF THE DEEP PACIFIC, WRAPPING ITS TENTACLES AROUND THE FISHING LINE.
It had taken the bait! Nearly 3,000 feet (900 m) above on the ocean's surface, Japanese scientists began reeling the beast—an elusive giant squid—into their research vessel. The creature tussled with the hook before finally breaking free, severing one of its tentacles in the battle. When the scientists hauled the appendage into the boat, they were startled to see it still wriggling! The 18-foot (5.5-m) tentacle slithered across the deck before latching onto a scientist's arm with teeth-lined suckers.

This encounter happened in 2004, but many of the details would sound familiar to sailors centuries ago. Ancient mariners feared the Kraken, a tentacled beast said to wreck ships and drag crewmen to their doom. Accounts from the 18th century describe a creature large enough to be mistaken for an island. Sailors off the coast of Africa claimed a Kraken wrapped its tentacles around their vessel and began pulling it under. Wielding cutlasses, the crew hacked off the tentacles and narrowly saved their ship.

But while yesterday's mariners dreaded a Kraken encounter, today's marine biologists would do anything to see one up close. They suspect that the giant squid—known by the scientific name *Architeuthis dux*—is the inspiration for the Kraken legend. As big as a school bus, this true sea titan prowls the lightless depths of the ocean preying on other squids and even whales.

Until recently, scientists had never seen a living giant squid. They only knew it existed from *Architeuthis* carcasses that washed up on beaches (the longest ever found measured 59 feet, or 18 meters). The Japanese scientists who tussled with the creature in 2004 reeled in a living specimen two years later. The 24-foot (7-m) beast "put up quite a fight" as they hauled it aboard. And it was only a baby.

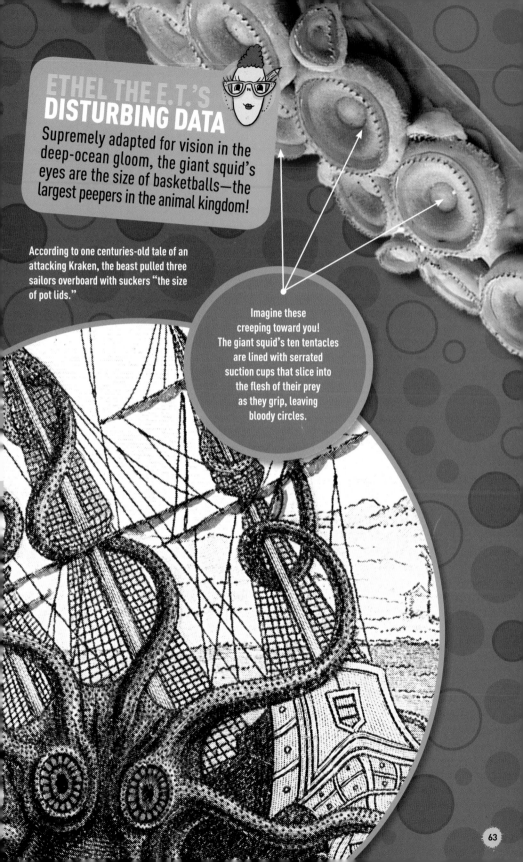

ETHEL THE E.T.'S DISTURBING DATA

Supremely adapted for vision in the deep-ocean gloom, the giant squid's eyes are the size of basketballs—the largest peepers in the animal kingdom!

According to one centuries-old tale of an attacking Kraken, the beast pulled three sailors overboard with suckers "the size of pot lids."

Imagine these creeping toward you! The giant squid's ten tentacles are lined with serrated suction cups that slice into the flesh of their prey as they grip, leaving bloody circles.

Shore

When "GLOBSTERS" ride in with the tide...

A BLOB OF BONELESS BLUBBER IS HARDLY THE SORT OF VISITOR YOU'D WANT CRASHING YOUR BEACH BARBECUE, but such stinky masses of decomposing tissue have washed ashore all over the world. Often mistaken for sea monsters, these so-called globsters make waves in the news and keep scientists guessing. Read all about the six famous specimens you wouldn't want washing up near your potato salad.

THE CHILEAN BLOB (CHILE, 2003)
Scientists were stumped when this 12-ton (10,886-kg) glob of pink-and-gray goo—nearly half the size of a tennis court—washed ashore on the southern coast of Chile. Study of its tissue revealed the Chilean Blob was the remains of a sperm whale, dashing scientists' hopes that they'd finally gotten the legendary giant octopus by the tentacle.

THE GIANT OARFISH
(SAN DIEGO, CALIFORNIA, U.S.A., 1996)
Not technically a globster—but no less a sea monster—this 23-foot (7-m) giant oarfish washed ashore in California. The world's largest bony fish, giant oarfish spend their lives prowling the lightless depths of the ocean. It's easy to see why dead oarfish are mistaken for sea serpents when they wash up on the sand.

Things

ST. AUGUSTINE MONSTER
(FLORIDA, U.S.A., 1896)

This blubbery mass is one of the first recorded examples of a beached blob. Was it the flesh of the fabled giant octopus? A castaway Kraken? Some sea creature new to science? A century later, scientists figured out that the St. Augustine Monster was actually the rotting body of a whale.

TASMANIAN GLOBSTER (TASMANIA, 1960)

"Nearly as Big as a House!" read a headline in a Tasmanian newspaper after this shapeless 10-ton (9,072-kg) mass rode in with the tide in western Tasmania. The term "globster" was coined to describe the blob, said to be covered with bristles and sprouting tusklike spikes instead of a mouth. The Tasmanian Globster was later identified as a whale carcass.

ZUIYO MARU CARCASS (NEW ZEALAND, 1977)

The crew of the Japanese fishing trawler *Zuiyo Maru* caught more than they bargained for when they hauled aboard a mysterious sea monster off the New Zealand coast. Noting its apparent slender neck and four finned limbs, Japanese scientists believed the carcass might be that of a plesiosaur, the extinct marine dinosaur often associated with the Loch Ness Monster and other lake monsters. Analysis showed it was the remains of a basking shark, which resembles a plesiosaur when it rots.

MEET THE
Montauk MONSTER

A CELEBRITY in the world of washed-up carcasses, the Montauk Monster became a media sensation after it was discovered above the high-tide mark at a popular tourist beach in July 2008. The mottled body appeared to sport a fanged beak, freaky humanlike fingers, and some sort of tag on its forelimb. The beach's proximity to an animal-disease testing center led to speculation that the Montauk Monster was actually an escaped lab animal that underwent mutating experiments, although most wildlife experts agree that it was just a dead raccoon. The creature became such a gruesome sensation that now the media labels any mysterious beached carcass a "Montauk Monster," no matter where it washes ashore.

SPOOKY SPOT

LATER IN THIS BOOK, YOU CAN READ ABOUT THE BERMUDA TRIANGLE, THAT MYSTERIOUS PATCH OF ATLANTIC OCEAN NOTORIOUS FOR SWALLOWING PLANES AND SHIPS. Head north over the Eastern United States for a thousand miles and you'll find another mysterious triangle that's similarly eerie except for one key difference: Things here tend to appear instead of disappear.

Welcome to the Bridgewater Triangle, a region in south-eastern Massachusetts, U.S.A., that pupils of the paranormal believe is a magnet for supernatural shenanigans. The Triangle takes shape when you connect the towns of Abington, Freetown, and Rehoboth on a map. Between them lies Hockomock Swamp, a soggy stretch of foggy marshes, sinister thickets, black rivers, and syrupy quicksand. Called "the place where the spirits dwell" by its original Native American inhabitants, Hockomock might be the world's creepiest picnic spot.

Here, residents claim they've encountered an all-star cast of supernatural creatures—from moaning ghosts to monster dogs to pterodactyls right out of *Jurassic Park.* Tragic events have occurred within the Traingle's boundaries, and some believe the swamp radiates an evil curse. It's no wonder the first English settlers named it "Devil's Swamp"!

TERRORS *of the* TRIANGLE

BIGFEET

People have reported seeing humanlike apes roaming the Triangle region. Hey, it's as good a place as any for a mythical monster!

THUNDERBIRDS

Swooping out of Native American mythology, these very big birds reportedly patrol the skies above Hockomock Swamp. One policeman claims he spotted a bird with a wingspan wider than two grown men!

PUKWUDGIES

Despite their wee stature—no taller than a fire hydrant—these troll-like creatures caused big trouble in Native American folklore, even luring people to their deaths. Witnesses say Pukwudgies are still up to their old tricks in the Triangle.

UFOS

The region has been a hotspot for UFO sightings ever since the 1700s. On Halloween night in 1908, two undertakers saw what looked like a lantern swoop over Hockomock Swamp. Which begs the question: Why would anyone go near Hockomock Swamp on Halloween night?!

WILL-O'-THE-WISPS

Some believe these ghostly balls of fire, typically seen in boggy areas, are the wandering spirits of the dearly departed. Scientists chalk them up to natural causes.

Unicorns
Are Real...

AND OTHER LIVING LEGENDS

DRAGONS DO EXIST!

Draco lizards of Southeast Asia glide between trees using wings of skin stretched over their extra-long ribs. These real-life dragons would be scary if they could breathe fire—and weren't small enough to become bird food!

ARAGOG SPINS HIS WEB!

Students of witchcraft and wizardry will recall the gargantuan arachnid Aragog and his titanic web in *Harry Potter and the Chamber of Secrets*. A similarly creepy scene greeted visitors to Texas, U.S.A.'s Lake Tawakoni State Park in 2007, when millions of baby spiders spun a web that spanned trees and walking paths. The silk spectacle attracted more than 3,000 visitors over a holiday weekend. We're assuming none of them suffered from arachnophobia—the fear of spiders.

MERMAIDS AREN'T JUST MAKE-BELIEVE!

Noting that they were "not half as beautiful as they are painted," Christopher Columbus spotted three "mermaids" while sailing for the New World in 1493. Turns out they were manatees, marine mammals occasionally mistaken for mermaids by sailors who've clearly been too long at sea.

UNICORNS ARE MORE THAN MYTHICAL!

Magical horned horses roam the realms of fairy tales, but deer and other antlered animals are occasionally born with a single horn in the real world. Such rare animals could have inspired the unicorn legend ages ago.

HOTEL TRANSYLVANIA: Count Dracula opens a resort for monsters only and invites the world's most famous frightening faces, from Frankenstein to a mummy to an entire family of werewolves. But the Count's worst nightmare comes true when a mortal man visits the hotel and falls for his 118-year-old daughter. See, even bloodthirsty fiends are afraid of something!

MONSTERS UNIVERSITY: This prequel to *Monsters, Inc.* is a must-watch if you've ever been afraid of scary creatures hiding under your bed. The movie follows two young monsters who go to college and major in scaring—an important skill in a world that harvests the screams of children for energy. See, monsters aren't mean. They just want to power their TVs and toasters!

MONSTERS
MAKING NICE

HARRY AND THE HENDERSONS: Bigfoot becomes the world's hairiest houseguest after family man George Henderson accidentally hits the creature with his station wagon. The Hendersons must nurse their furry new friend—whom they name Harry—while hiding him from nosy neighbors and a determined big game hunter. Along the way, we learn that Bigfoots (Bigfeet?) bury their dead and are experts at hiding in plain sight. So that's why they're so hard to find!

LEGENDARY Creatures

AIIIIEEEE!	Chupacabra
TERRIFYING	Montauk Monster
SPINE-TINGLING	Kraken
	Pukwudgies
UNSETTLING	Sasquatch
	Loch Ness Monster

PhEAR FACTOR

PHENOMENA ELICITING ABNORMAL REACTIONS

Agent Jeeper Ranks **CREEPY CRYPTOIDS.**

CHAPTER 4

Witchcraft
and Wizardry

WITCHES AND WIZARDS ARE SUPER-HEROES TODAY—THANKS TO THE SPELLBINDING ADVENTURES OF HARRY POTTER AND HIS PALS—BUT IT WASN'T ALWAYS THAT WAY. Suspected practitioners of magic were once feared rather than celebrated, and no chants or potions could save the poor souls who became the targets of witch hunts. Hop aboard your comfiest broom as we soar through the scary history of spells, curses, and the people who cast them. It's the next best thing to taking a history class at Hogwarts!

WITCHES' WOE

"CUNNING FOLK" ON TRIAL

"DOUBLE, DOUBLE, TOIL AND TROUBLE; FIRE BURN AND CAULDRON BUBBLE." So goes the famous witches' chant from William Shakespeare's *Macbeth*. The English poet wrote the play in the early 1600s, when every witch was considered public enemy number one. Macbeth's witches are filthy hags, stooped over a bad brew of human organs, dragon scales, and eye of newt.

It's hardly a fair portrayal. Witches were once viewed as valuable members of their communities. Known as "cunning folk" or "wise women" (although men were witches, too), they relied on their knowledge of the natural world to mix medicines, cast out evil spirits, deliver babies, and occasionally whip up potions for people unlucky in love. But by the 15th century, Europe had become a dangerous place for cunning folk. Church officials linked witchcraft to the devil, claiming that all witches drew their power from evil. Meanwhile, plagues, failed crops, and wars spread misery across Europe. People looked for someone to blame, and witches became the target.

After all, according to folklore and books written at the time, witches possessed all sorts of evil powers. They could ruin crops, curdle the milk of livestock, blot out the stars, control the weather, and curse their neighbors. Anyone suffering a run of rotten luck could blame it on a witch. Such hysteria—or out-of-control fear and panic—spread across northern Europe and even to the new colonies in North America. Suspected witches were rounded up, tortured into confessing any number of unnatural crimes, then burned alive at the stake. By the 1700s, as many as 60,000 suspected witches had been tried and executed in Europe.

Eventually, reason prevailed and witch hysteria became a shameful part of European and American history. The practice of witchcraft today is known as Wicca. Modern-day cunning folk mix potions and cast spells in hidden forest meadows and at secret gatherings, far from prying eyes.

MEET A FAMOUS WITCH: ISOBEL GOWDIE

Unlike the thousands of innocent women who were tortured into confessing their practice of witchcraft, in 1662 red-headed Scottish housewife Isobel Gowdie freely admitted to being a witch. She claimed she had joined a company of 13 witches—a group known as a "coven"—who tormented fellow villagers by ruining their crops and summoning storms. They passed the time by transforming into animals and casting hexes on children. Despite Gowdie's bold admission, there's no record of her being executed for witchcraft.

MEET A FAMOUS WITCH HUNTER: MATTHEW HOPKINS

After claiming that a group of witches tried to kill him in 1644, this Englishman declared himself Witchfinder General and began traveling the countryside on the hunt for sorcerers. His interrogation methods were nothing short of brutal. Hopkins would prick suspected witches with pins and keep them awake until they confessed. By the end of his career in 1647, he was responsible for as many as 230 executions. Some believe Hopkins himself was accused of and put to death for witchcraft.

THE SALEM WITCH HUNT

One of the most famous witch trials took place in Salem Village (now Danvers, Massachusetts, U.S.A.) in the 1690s. It started when a group of young girls began suffering from bizarre fits. They blamed a West Indian slave named Tituba for teaching them witchcraft, and soon the list of suspected witches grew to include other villagers, including men and a six-year-old child. The ensuing witch craze cost the lives of 20 people. Scholars suspect the girls who started the hysteria were simply looking for attention. Another possibility: A fungus in the town's food supply may have caused hallucinations of bewitchment.

YOU MIGHT'VE BEEN ACCUSED OF

witchcraft if...

AGENT JEEPER'S
REALITY CHECK

Look over these signs of witchcraft again and think of all the people in your life they might describe. They could apply to anybody, right? So when you read about the thousands of supposed witches put on trial in the 15th through 17th centuries, remember: They weren't sinister sorcerers wielding black magic. They were simply victims of hysteria and fear, trapped in a no-win situation.

...YOU WERE LEFT-HANDED

Being a southpaw is no picnic nowadays, what with everything from power tools to computer mice made for righties. But in the age of witch hunts, lefties lived under constant suspicion. Left-handedness was seen as an insult to the natural order of things and a sign of evil. In fact, the term "sinister" comes from the Latin word for left.

...YOU BORE THE WITCH'S MARK

Witches were thought to soar on broomsticks to "Sabbaths," rowdy assemblies of sorcerers deep in the forest. At these sinister shindigs, the devil would initiate beginning spellcasters by scarring them with his horns. His "witch's mark" could take the shape of an animal—perhaps a cat or toad—or look like a birthmark. Accused witches underwent head-to-toe inspections for such markings.

...YOU SANK INSTEAD OF FLOATED

One test for a suspected sorcerer was to tie him or her to a chair and toss it into a river. Genuine witches—supposedly immune to the holy power of baptism in water—would bob to the surface. Thus proven guilty, they were usually executed. Those innocent of witchcraft would sink instead of float. They often drowned! In other words, this test meant death regardless of its results.

...YOU WERE AT LEAST 40 YEARS OLD

Folks in their 40s are considered middle-aged today, but few people reached such a ripe old age in the 14th and 15th centuries. Those who did were suspected of consorting with evil powers to achieve such a freakishly long life span.

...YOU'D HAD A FALLING-OUT

At the height of the witch panics, people were encouraged to report suspected witches to religious officials and witch hunters. That gave anyone with a grievance the opportunity to get even. They could accuse anyone they didn't like of witchcraft!

...YOU NEVER CRIED

According to the *Malleus Maleficarum*, the 15th-century encyclopedia of witch hunting also known as the *Hammer of Witches*, those guilty of witchcraft never shed a tear. Even if they appeared to sob while undergoing torturous interrogations, the book said, they were only pretending to cry. Just goes to show: Witch trials were not fair!

MALLEI
MALEFICARVM
TRACTATVS ALIQVOT
TAM VETERVM, QVAM
Recentiorum in vnum corpus congestum,
ARTIS MAGICÆ STVPENDOS AFFECTVS,
Lamiarum Pytionissae contraetus, lupia degmata, sporticias,
festinationes, venefiisque demostrantis,
TOMI SECVNDI PARS PRIOR.
Cum INDICIBVS Auctorum & rerum verisimilis.

NAME **CRP003** SOLVED

Creepy Case File #3: Black Magic Academy

SUBJECT: The Scholomance, a supposed school of witchcraft and wizardry

LOCATION: The mountains south of Sibiu, Romania

TIME FRAME: 900 B.C. to A.D. 1900

CASE BACKGROUND:

It's a familiar setting for any Harry Potter fan: a supernatural school on the shore of a bottomless lake, somewhere deep in the mountains. But this particular magical academy isn't Hogwarts, and "the boy who lived" wouldn't be caught dead here. The Scholomance, as this school is known, was home to a far less heroic pupil: Count Dracula. The school was said to exist in the heart of Transylvania. Its headmaster was the devil himself, and he taught everything from forbidden spells to the languages of animals. It was an exclusive academy—just ten pupils were admitted at a time. When their education in the dark arts was complete, nine alumni were allowed to return home. The tenth remained at the school to become the devil's assistant. Saddled on a dragon, the assistant would conjure storms and hurl bolts of lightning. When thunderstorms rumbled across the Carpathian Mountains, everyone knew class was in session.

WAS **TRANSYLVANIA** HOME TO A REAL-LIFE **HOGWARTS?**

Hunting for Hogwarts...

ALNWICK CASTLE

This sprawling English castle served as the backdrop for Hogwarts in the first two Harry Potter movies. It was built late in the 11th century and survived several sieges.

THE ALCHEMY MUSEUM

Descend the stone staircase to the basement of this medieval building in Kutná Hora, Czech Republic, and you'd swear you had walked into Professor Snape's classroom. Here, curator Michal Pober demonstrated the tools and techniques of ancient chemistry.

GREY SCHOOL OF WIZARDRY

Wannabe witches and wizards only need a Web connection to attend this virtual school, which offers majors in healing, beast mastery—even the dark arts!

CASE ANALYSIS:

Scottish writer Emily Gerard introduced the world to the Scholomance in an 1885 article about Transylvanian superstitions. According to her, the academy existed somewhere in the mountains south of modern-day Sibiu, Romania. Dracula author Bram Stoker used Gerard's article as research for his famous book. He wrote that Dracula "dared even to attend the Scholomance, and there was no branch of knowledge of his time that he did not essay."

But was the Scholomance a real school? The word didn't exist until Gerard's article. Folklorists believe she may have confused the school's name for an ancient order of wizards from Romanian folklore known as the Solomanari. Like the students in Gerard's sinister school, the Solomanari were said to ride dragons and control the weather. Whether they played games of Quidditch is anyone's guess.

79

BROOM

Believing the year's crops would grow to the height of their heartiest leaps, ancient witches straddled their brooms and bounded through the fields. Brooms have been linked to witch transportation ever since. Typically, witches hop aboard with the straw end down. In the late 17th century, however, people thought witches rode with the bristles facing upward (and with a candle mounted in the straw as a sort of headlight). If you see a witch who appears to be flying backward in an old illustration, now you know why!

PENTACLE

A powerful symbol among witches, this circled pentagram (or star shape) serves as both a protective shield and a tool for focusing magical energy. Witches wear the pentacle (pronounced "pen-tickle") as a charm and trace it on objects intended for enchantment.

FAMILIAR

Meet a witch's best friend. Familiars are magical creatures in the shape of common animals, such as toads, rabbits, owls, and especially black cats. Witches treat their familiars as beloved pets. In return, the creatures help their caretakers cast spells. A 17th-century witch named Elizabeth Clark claimed she had five familiars, including a rabbit named Sack and Sugar.

ATHAME

Witches wield this knife (pronounced "ah-tha-may") to trace spell symbols and prepare potion ingredients. It's never used as a weapon. Witches who want more ceremonial oomph carry a sword instead.

GRIMOIRE

A witch never leaves home without this spellbook (pronounced "grim-wah"). It contains page after page of potion recipes, charm-construction instructions, and secret illustrations for casting spells. Sometimes, the grimoire itself is enchanted with magical powers.

MAGIC WAND

Magical rods have been around since the days of Greek mythology. Witches and wizards wield them to channel their inner power. A wand can be crafted from any number of materials, from gold to crystal. Some witches believe the best wands are carved from hazelwood during a full moon.

CREEPY EQUIPMENT

WITCHES' WARES

THINK WIZARDS AND WITCHES CONJURE MAGIC FROM THIN AIR?

Well, supposedly they do! But according to folklore they also summon it from the other elements: water, fire, and earth. They are said to harness it from nature and pray for power from gods and goddesses, such as the "Horned God" of the wilderness. And to make the most of this magic, wizards and witches rely on a variety of tools . . . .

CAULDRON
Witches brew their potions, poisons, and ointments in this heavy iron pot.

BEWITCHING BREWS

POTENT **POTIONS** FROM **WITCHCRAFT** LORE

FLYING OINTMENT

A witch needed more than just a sleek broom to rocket into the night; she had to smear her skin with a magical ointment to obtain the power of flight. Flying-ointment recipes from the 16th century called for animal fat (sometimes the fat of children!) and herbs known to invoke visions. Scholars believe these powerful potions invoked visions of flight rather than actual air travel. In fact, one modern-day researcher who cooked up flying ointment claimed it sent him into a deep slumber full of vivid dreams of flight and feasting.

LOVE POTION

Also known as a "philtre" (pronounced "fil-ter"), the love potion was a common enchantment going back to ancient times. Ingredients included the toxic mandrake root, animal organs, and a dash of fruit or fragrance to cover the bad smell. The potion wasn't ready to drink until it was mixed with wine or tea. Whoever chugged it fell head over heels for the person who served it, so great care had to be taken to ensure the potion reached its intended target. Otherwise things could get . . . awkward.

CLOAKING LOTION

Like a messier version of Harry Potter's invisibility cloak, this greasy concoction was supposed to magically camouflage wizards and witches if they applied it from head to toe. Witches in the Middle Ages used cloaking lotions to sneak from their homes and attend secret Sabbaths.

METAMORPHOSIS OINTMENT

Witches are well known for turning people into newts and toads, but they were also quick-change artists themselves, able to transform into owls, cats, crows, insects, and wolves. Metamorphosis lotions contained powerful mind-altering substances just as flying ointments did. Witches who applied the ointments may not have transformed into birds and beasts—but they certainly believed they did!

Active
Ingredients

NIGHTSHADE: A family of flowering plants that includes belladonna and mandrake, nightshades could relieve pain, cause delusions, or kill, depending on the species and amount used.

HEMLOCK:
A deadly plant, popular among witches for killing potions.

WOLFSBANE: This toxic flower was plucked from mountain meadows and used in transformation potions. It also goes by the name "Dumbledore's Delight." (*Dumbledore* is an old word for "bumblebee.")

LARD: Witches added fat as a greasy base for their ointments. This fat didn't always come from animals . . .

PINS: Crooked pins twisted the effects of potions, turning them evil. Superstitious people picked up any stray pins so witches couldn't use them.

Bizarre BAZ

Shop till you're shocked at the TOGO VOODOO MARKET, **the**

YOU SMELL THE PLACE BEFORE YOU SEE IT. Here in Lomé, capital of the West
African country of Togo, a sweet-and-sour stink hangs over the dusty streets. Your nose leads you on a grim safari. Tables overflow with teetering stacks of antelope skulls, grinning crocodile jaws, and dried monkey paws, all baking in the African sun. These

grisly goods share shelf space with amulets, carved dolls, and mysterious elixirs—essential ingredients for voodoo witchcraft.

And it's all for sale.

You've stumbled into the Togo Voodoo Market. It's a real-life Diagon Alley, the bustling district of supernatural shops from the world of Harry Potter. Practitioners of

Skulls, skins, and bones of hundreds of birds and beasts lie in stacked rows organized by species. Voodoo practitioners mix them with herbs and burn them into black ash—a potent potion ingredient.

AAR

world's freakiest pharmacy!

voodoo—a ritual-rich religion that originated here in West Africa—trek to Togo when they run low on spare animal parts, rare herbs, and other exotic ingredients for magical cures and spells. Patients and tourists alike can visit the local voodoo priest for love potions, good-luck charms, and remedies for any illness. (A typical cure for asthma includes porcupine quills mashed with boa constrictor spines.) Don't bother looking for price tags; shopkeepers set the cost of each transaction by tossing tiny bones.

Despite the ghastly goods on display, curious customers have little to fear while they browse: The market's minders promise they don't dabble in black magic.

To nonbelievers, the Togo Voodoo Market might seem like a shocking collection of shops, but to the 30 million West Africans who practice voodoo, it's just another drugstore.

In the market for a voodoo doll? A love potion? A statue that provides home security? Togo's stalls have it all.

THE TROUBLE WITH TUT

Mess with a mummy at your own risk! Tomb walls in ancient Egypt were inscribed with spells to frighten away grave robbers. "To all who enter to make evil against this tomb," read one inscription, "may the crocodile be against them on water and the snakes and scorpions be against them on land." Indeed, tragedy tracked the discovery of King Tut's grave by archaeologist Howard Carter in 1922. When the sponsor of the Tut expedition, Lord Carnarvon, died less than a year after the tomb was opened, reporters pounced on the idea that he'd fallen victim to a mummy's curse. It wasn't crocs or scorpions that did in Lord Carnarvon, however. He died from an infected mosquito bite.

A DEADLY DIAMOND

t's been worn by kings and queens, swiped by jewel thieves, and was once feared lost in a shipwreck. No rock has a richer history than the Hope Diamond, although most people know it for one reason: It's supposedly cursed! Legend has it that the diamond—the largest of its kind— was pried from an ancient Hindu idol by a treasure hunter who later regretted t. (He was eaten alive by wolves!) The tale s almost certainly untrue, although many of the stone's wners didn't live happily ever after. King Louis XVI lost his head in the French Revolution. More than a hundred years ater, a woman who wore the diamond became convinced it was cursed after her husband, eldest son, and daughter ll died. She refused to sell the stone for fear of passing long the curse, and it was later donated to the Smithsonian nstitution. Visit its exhibit if you dare.

CURSES!

FAMOUS CASES OF HORRIBLE HEXES . . . .

BAD-NEWS BOG

You'd expect to see a spirit or three skulking about the alligator-infested wilderness outside New Orleans, allegedly America's most ghost-infested city. But Louisiana's Manchac Swamp delivers a deluxe combo of creepiness in its soggy moss-draped expanse—it's haunted and cursed! According to legend, a voodoo priestess cast a hex upon the swamp's residents, promising that she would take them all with her when she passed away. Sure enough, on the day of her funeral in 1915, a hurricane tore through the swamp, drowning hundreds. Whether the storm washed away the curse is unknown.

HEAD FOR THE HILL

Unless you're frightened of frolicking deer or beautiful fall foliage, Hexenkopf Hill in eastern Pennsylvania, U.S.A., isn't a particularly scary place during the day. But you might want to steer clear of this rocky mountain at night—especially once you know the history of this spot. *Hexenkopf* is German for "Witch's Head," and legend has it that witches once gathered on its summit for Sabbaths. One resident witch cursed her neighbors for meddling with her affairs, so they hanged her for practicing magic. Her ghost is said to still wander the hill, eager to hex the living. When the hill casts an eerie glow at night, it means the witches have returned. (Or perhaps it's just the mica minerals in the rocks glinting in the moonlight, but where's the fun in that?)

GHASTLY GOOD-LUCK CHARMS

SPIDERS: Next time you feel the urge to squish an icky arachnid, consider this: Spotting a spider is a good thing in many cultures. According to Native American mythology, for instance, a giant spider weaved the world. In France, it's considered good luck to see a spider before you tuck yourself in at night.

SNAKES: Don't feel bad if snakes make you squirm—even whip-cracking tough guy Indiana Jones hates those slithering reptiles. In parts of China, however, finding a snake in your house brings good luck. White snakes in Japan serve as a symbol of big bucks.

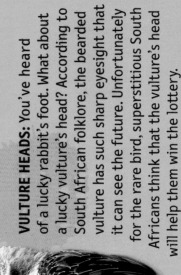

VULTURE HEADS: You've heard of a lucky rabbit's foot. What about a lucky vulture's head? According to South African folklore, the bearded vulture has such sharp eyesight that it can see the future. Unfortunately for the rare bird, superstitious South Africans think that the vulture's head will help them win the lottery.

WORLD OF *Witchcraft*

Witch Hunts — **AIIIIEEEE!**

Curses — **TERRIFYING**

Hammer of Witches — **SPINE-TINGLING**

The Scholomance — **UNSETTLING**

Togo Voodoo Market

PhEAR FACTOR

PHENOMENA ELICITING ABNORMAL REACTIONS

Ethel the E.T. Ranks **MAGICAL MATTERS.**

CHAPTER 5

Spirits Rising

WHAT'S THAT SPOOKY NOISE IN THE NIGHT? IS IT THE WIND? DOES THE CAT WANT IN? OR IS IT... SOMETHING ELSE? THERE'S NO SHAME IN SUSPECTING A SPECTER! After all, history is alive with tales of the restless dead, and even the ancient Egyptians believed in ghosts. In this chapter, you'll meet a who's who of things that go boo, including famous phantoms and even some paranormal pets. Are ghostly apparitions really the remnants of our dearly departed or just all in our heads? Turn the page to see if the spirits move you...

The Story of GHOSTS

Stuffed animals and bits of candy spill from a shelf in a dim room beneath the city of Edinburgh, Scotland. Here, in this spooky underground neighborhood known as Mary King's Close, tourists come bearing gifts for a sad girl named Annie, said to wander the underground streets and homes. Whether she appreciates this pile of presents is up for debate. According to legend, Annie died of the plague more than three centuries ago.

Call them specters, spooks, phantoms, or spirits—they're all different names for the same phenomenon: ghosts. Paranormal investigators believe ghosts are the spirits of people who have passed away yet remain stuck in our world. Restless and confused, they haunt the houses where they lived and the places where they died. The specter of sad little Annie, for instance, is said to wander the room in which she was locked away to expire from her illness.

Spectral activity takes many forms: creepy moans, creaky stairs, flickering lights, sudden chills, shadowy figures, and even fully formed apparitions dressed in old-fashioned getups. Using high-tech gadgets, pursuers of the paranormal skulk through old houses, graveyards, and other allegedly haunted spots hoping to document ghostly goings-on. They've yet to uncover any conclusive evidence, but that hardly seems to matter. A third of all Americans claim they believe in ghosts. And visitors to Mary King's Close are happy to leave toys and treats, hoping they'll raise the spirits of a ghostly girl.

THREE SPECIES OF SPIRITS

INTELLIGENT APPARITION

his type of ghost seems aware f his or her environment nd will even interact with ne living. You might strike p a creepy conversation ith one—if you don't flee n terror first.

NE GHOST'S STORY: A young an named Jerry Palus met a retty woman at a Chicago J.S.A.)-area hall in 1939. As he wirled her around the dance oor, Palus couldn't help oticing the woman's cold ands and distant demeanor. ne asked for a ride to esurrection Cemetery— nly to vanish as she glided nrough the gates. "Resurrec- on Mary" has haunted earby roads ever since.

RESIDUAL APPARITION

Think of this haunting as a scary movie stuck on repeat. The specter relives a particular event—often related to his or her gruesome death—over and over without taking notice of any observers.

ONE GHOST'S STORY: Tourists who visit Gettysburg, a famous— and famously haunted—Civil War battlefield in Pennsylvania, U.S.A., report seeing the specters of soldiers reenacting the brutal battle. Entire platoons of spooky troops wield phantom rifles and ride ghostly horses.

CRISIS APPARITION

This friendly ghost material- izes only to warn the living— often the spirit's friends and family—of impending danger or just to bid farewell.

ONE GHOST'S STORY: An owner of a New Jersey, U.S.A., hair salon was closing up shop in 2001 when one of her custom- ers dropped by to tell her thanks for everything. The next day, the salon owner learned that the customer was found dead nine hours before their chat!

GHOST
Gallery

GHOST BUSTED

Security guards weren't sure what tripped a door alarm at London's Hampton Court Palace, a 16th-century home for King Henry VIII. The guards found the door closed and everything A-OK—until they reviewed the security tape. The grainy footage showed the doors popping open on their own, then being pulled shut by a creepy cloaked figure. The ghost was later dubbed "Skeletor."

STAIRWAY TO HEAVEN

A retired couple from Canada photographed this staircase in 1966 while touring the Queen's House, a 17th-century royal residence in Greenwich, England. When they returned home and had the picture developed, they were shocked to see two (or is it three?!) veiled figures ascending the stairs while clutching the handrail. Apparently, even apparitions play it safe on the stairs!

POSE IN THESE FAMOUS PHOTOS …

THE LEGLESS LORD

Amateur photographer Sybell Corbet thought she was alone when she snapped this picture in the library of an English abbey in 1891. Once developed, the photo revealed the wispy image of a legless elderly gentleman kicking back in a chair. Some believed the man was Lord Combermere, the lord of the abbey. There was just one problem: At the time the photo was taken, the lord was being laid to rest at his funeral a few miles away. He had died in an accident that would have rendered his legs useless.

AGENT JEEPER
Claims Ghosts Are Bogus!

Researchers have determined that all sorts of normal phenomena—electrical fields, low-frequency sounds, and even fear itself—can cause feelings of unease and lead to hallucinations of hauntings.

ETHEL THE E.T.
Swears Ghosts Are Real!

Paranormal investigators believe that people leave behind energy when they die—especially when they die a traumatic death—and that this energy manifests itself as spectral activity.

GHOST
Gallery
(CONTINUED)

SPECTER OF THE SCOTTISH CASTLE

When Professor Richard Wiseman, a skeptic of the paranormal, ran a contest in 2009 to find the most convincing phantom photo, this creepy picture nabbed first place. Taken at the ruins of a Scottish medieval fortress known as Tantallon Castle, it appears to show a lady wearing a 16th-century neck ruffle peering from a barred window. Was she simply a visitor in a medieval mood . . . or one of the castle's original residents?

FREE SPIRIT

A mischievous-looking schoolgirl in old-fashioned duds peeks through the smoke in this 1995 photo of a town hall fire in the English village of Wem. Locals believed the picture showed the ghost of a naughty little girl who had set fire to the town in 1677, but skeptics think she was cropped into the image from a 1922 postcard. Fake or not, the "Wem Ghost" still raises goose bumps.

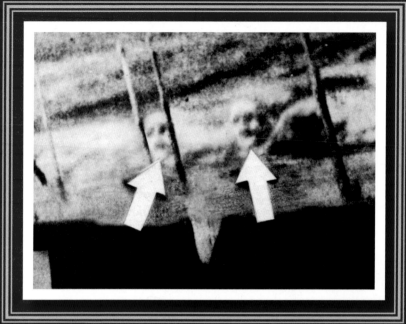

FLOATING PHANTOMS

After succumbing to fumes aboard their ship, two crewmen of the oil tanker S.S. *Watertown* were given a burial at sea—but their fellow sailors hadn't seen the last of them. Whenever the tanker returned to Pacific waters, the dead men's faces would haunt the ship from the waves. The *Watertown*'s captain snapped this famous photo of the phantom faces in 1925, although skeptics think it's an obvious fake.

The TALKING DEAD

DO THE DEARLY DEPARTED REALLY CHAT WITH MEDIUMS?

"Dead men tell no tales," the old saying goes. Mediums would beg to differ! These are people who claim a special connection with the spirit world, able to act as messengers between the dead and the living. Some mediums enter a trance to let the dead speak through them, often in a low or strained voice (a creepy process known as "channeling"). They might arrange a "séance," in which loved ones gather in a gloomy room and pepper the medium with questions for their dearly departed. "Is Uncle Hank happy in the hereafter?" they might ask. "Oh, and where did he leave the Blu-ray remote?"

Although mediums have offered their spooky services since ancient times, scientists are skeptical of their supernatural powers. The Fox Sisters, a trio of 19th-century mediums who became famous for eliciting strange rapping sounds from the dead, were revealed as frauds (they were making the knocking noises with their feet and knuckles). Escape artist Harry Houdini used his expertise in sleight of hand to debunk many supposed mediums—a crusade he continued after his death. Houdini's wife challenged mediums to discover a secret code that only she and her husband had shared. Determined mediums held séances each Halloween (the anniversary of Houdini's death) for ten years after he died, but the secret words were never revealed. Either the mediums were all phonies, or Houdini's spirit was keeping mum.

CREEPY EQUIPMENT

Ghost-Hunting Gear

FIVE SENSES ARE INSUFFICIENT FOR PEOPLE WHO PURSUE THE PARANORMAL. Things that go bump in the night rarely appear in plain sight, and eerie sensations—from goose bumps to the heebie-jeebies—aren't exactly hard evidence of the supernatural. To extend their sensory powers and evidence-recording capabilities, ghost hunters arm themselves with an array of sophisticated gadgets that detect phenomena outside the range of human vision and hearing. Here's a gadget-by-gadget guide to the cool tools of specter inspection...

DIGITAL CAMERA

Snap, snap, snap—ghost hunters typically take hundreds of pictures while investigating potential haunt spots. They'll scrutinize the shots and footage later to see if their cameras captured any eerie evidence. Well-heeled hunters use fancier cameras that capture phenomena invisible to the naked eye. These full-spectrum photographs look creepy even when they don't show alleged ghosts!

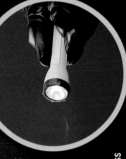

FLASHLIGHT

Nighttime is the right time to stalk spirits, so ghost hunters need a light to avoid bumbling around in the dark. Extra batteries are a good idea, too—unless you like the idea of skulking around a spooky spot in pitch blackness because your Duracells died.

IR THERMOMETER

Ever feel a sudden chill while strolling through a creepy house? Paranormal researchers believe that ghosts convert heat from the air into energy to make themselves seen or heard. An IR thermometer, which fires an invisible infrared beam to take the temperature of distant objects, can pinpoint cold spots for further investigation.

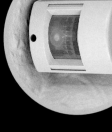

TAPE RECORDER/
DIGITAL RECORDER

Haunt hunters believe that ghosts make an eternal racket—moans, screams, snatches of conversation—that we humans can't hear. The only way to detect these "electronic voice phenomena" (EVP for short) is with a recording device. Ghost hunters painstakingly pore over their recordings to isolate these supernatural sounds. Alleged EVPs range from creepy sobs to bone-chilling screams.

MOTION DETECTOR

Think of this gadget as a ghost alarm. Its infrared sensor detects moving objects of an unusual temperature. Ghost hunters place these sensors throughout haunted locales to monitor multiple rooms. Triggered sensors emit shrill alarms that have ghost hunters running to the scene, hoping to catch a specter in mid-haunt.

EMF DETECTOR

This meter measures changes in electromagnetic fields—electrical energy generated by the volts joting through your microwave, fridge, television, and house wiring. Suspecting that specters also create these fields, paranormal investigators search for EMF hot spots far from electrical sources. High EMF readings can indicate a haunt is happening!

HEL THE E.T.'S
STURBING DATA

as Edison, inventor of the lightbulb,
ed he was working on a device for
nunicating with ghosts.

STAIR SCARE

The Brown Lady of Raynham Hall

"QUICK, QUICK! THERE'S SOMETHING!" exclaimed photographer Indre Shira to his colleague, Captain Provand. It was 1936, and the two were photographing the charming parlors and lavish furnishings of Raynham Hall, an old English manor. Provand was manning a camera pointed at the mansion's oak staircase. He saw nothing in the viewfinder but took the picture anyway, then turned to Shira and asked, "What's all the excitement about?"

Shira swore he'd seen a ghost! Sure enough, when the duo developed the photo, it revealed a shrouded, glowing apparition gliding down the staircase. There, caught on film, was the famous "Brown Lady," a specter known for knocking around Raynham Hall in a heavy brown dress since the 1800s. She was believed to be the ghost of Lady Dorothy Walpole, whose vengeful husband had locked her away for life after suspecting she had an affair. Hall residents who encountered the Brown Lady claimed she had sad eyes or—eek!—no eyes at all. One frightened guest even fired his pistol at the ghost. The shot passed right through her and into the wall.

Although it has its skeptics, Provand and Shira's photo has become the most famous phantom photo of all time. The Brown Lady, meanwhile, hasn't been seen since.

NAME **CRP004**

Creepy Case File #4: Keeper of the Crypt

SUBJECT: Black Aggie, an allegedly haunted graveside statue

LOCATION: Druid Ridge Cemetery, Maryland, U.S.A.

TIME FRAME: A.D. 1907 to present

CASE BACKGROUND:

It was a scary dare that lasted decades. Teenagers and college students sneaked into Maryland's Druid Ridge Cemetery in the dead of night to confront "Black Aggie," the local name for a spooky statue that guarded a gravesite. Some peeked under Aggie's bronze cowl to see if her eyes really glowed red. The most foolhardy sat in her lap, despite a tale of Aggie springing to life and crushing a college student to death.

The statue's legend spread among her midnight visitors. They said she sat atop the grave of a witch, whose vengeful spirit haunted her bronze figure. No grass grew in her shadow, and anyone who dared to meet her stare felt a sudden sense of dread. Then, in 1967, Black Aggie's legend took a terrifying twist when she disappeared from the cemetery. All that remained was a chipped smudge on the pedestal where she had sat vigil for 60 years. Had the haunted monument finally come to life?

DID A SINISTER
CEMETERY STATUE
WALK AWAY FROM
THE GRAVE?

Ghostly Graveyards

BACHELOR'S GROVE CEMETERY, Illinois, U.S.A.
This creepy country graveyard outside Chicago, Illinois, U.S.A., is lively with ghost sightings. The most famous: a lady dressed in white caught sitting on a tombstone.

STULL CEMETERY
The devil himself supposedly roams the graves of this Kansas, U.S.A., boneyard, considered by some to be a gateway to hell.

ST. LOUIS CEMETERY
New Orleans is said to be the most haunted city in America, so it's no surprise that the city's famous cemetery is a hot spot for ghostly activity, including moans from a supposed voodoo queen.

CASE ANALYSIS:

In 1907, a Civil War veteran and Baltimore newspaper publisher named Felix Agnus sought a memorial for his family's burial plot in Druid Ridge Cemetery. He liked the somber look of a statue that adorned the grave of Marian Adams, a woman who died under tragic circumstances in nearby Washington, D.C., so he commissioned a copy from a dealer in counterfeit sculptures. Agnus erected the cloned sculpture over his mother's grave, etching the family name into its pedestal (the inspiration for Black Aggie's nickname).

Years later, kids began daring each other to approach the scary statue at night.

In 1967, pressed by cemetery owners sick of teenagers trampling the grass, the Agnus family removed the statue. Today, Black Aggie sits in a courtyard not far from the White House. Government workers on lunch breaks nibble on sandwiches nearby, unaware of the statue's sinister history and unafraid to meet her gaze.

ETHEL THE E.T.'S DISTURBING DATA

Terrified of being buried alive, more and more people are insisting that their caskets come equipped with cell phones so they can call for help from the grave.

ATTACK OF THE
DEMON CAT
AND OTHER ENCOUNTERS WITH FURRY PHANTOMS

IT LOOKED LIKE ANY OTHER BLACK HOUSECAT—until it started growling . . . and growing. Startled, the security guard reached for his pistol. He had been halfway through his nightly rounds of the Capitol Building in Washington, D.C., U.S.A., when he stumbled upon the infamous "demon cat," a phantom feline said to prowl the building's basement since 1865. The snarling specter padded closer to the guard, increasing in size with each step. When it reached panther proportions, it pounced! The guard pulled his gun and fired, but the cat apparition vanished in midair.

According to paranormal investigators, not all ghosts are the spirits of restless people. Some phantoms walk on all fours. They're spectral pets that refuse to roll over and play dead, or the apparitions of wild animals haunting their old habitats. Washington, D.C.'s demon cat—called D.C. for short—is one of the most famous of these animal ghosts. Legend has it that when D.C. shows up, bad things are bound to happen. The cat was spotted before the assassinations of U.S. Presidents Abraham Lincoln and John F. Kennedy. It put in an appearance before the Stock Market Crash of 1929.

The Capitol had a serious rat problem in the early 1800s, and cats were brought in to control the infestation. Could D.C. be a specter of one of these wandering rat-catchers or just a stray? It's not easy telling one from the other when you're walking the Capitol's creepy depths at midnight.

THE WEASEL WRAITH

In the 1930s, reporters and paranormal investigators descended on a remote farmhouse on the Isle of Man to see something out of a twisted Saturday morning cartoon. The house's residents claimed they were visited by a talking mongoose named Gef, who'd introduced himself as a ghost in weasel form and even offered to help around the house.

BEST FRIEND FROM BEYOND

Not only did Hollywood heartthrob Rudolph Valentino become an often seen celebrity specter after his death in 1926, his faithful dog Kabar did, too. The Great Dane is said to haunt the Los Angeles, California, U.S.A., pet cemetery where he was buried. Visitors have heard him barking and panting. Some even claim Kabar's ghost licked them!

BAD-LUCK MUTT

The sudden appearance of a black dog—particularly at night—was seen as a sign of impending doom in the British Isles and elsewhere. Perhaps the most frightening dark dog of all belonged to the 17th-century ghost of Lady Mary Howard, said to ride through the English countryside in a horse-drawn carriage made of bones.

ETHEL THE E.T.'S DISTURBING DATA

When a man dies unmarried in north China, his family might buy the body of a young woman to serve as his wife in the afterlife. This ancient custom has spawned an illegal market in "ghost brides" snatched from graveyards.

SPOOKY SPOT

THE TOWER OF LONDON

WHEN WILLIAM THE CONQUEROR INVADED ENGLAND NEARLY A THOUSAND YEARS AGO, HE BUILT A WHITE TOWER IN LONDON TO STRIKE FEAR INTO HIS NEW SUBJECTS. Today, after centuries of expansion by William's heirs, the Tower of London still strikes fear in visitors and guards. Home to famous kings and queens, site of beheadings and torture, it's considered one of the most haunted castles in England. Here's a guide to its famous ghosts . . .

THE SCREAMING SPECTER

HAUNT SPOT: Tower Green

Description: Guards report hearing shrieks of agony echo across the castle's grounds.

Historical origin: After he was caught planning to blow up England's Parliament building in 1605, Guy Fawkes was tortured into revealing his partners in the plot, then executed.

TWO LITTLE PHANTOMS

HAUNT SPOT: Bloody Tower

Description: The ghosts of two sad-looking boys are said to haunt this tower. Guests have tried to console the children—only to see their spectral forms vanish into the wall.

Historical origin: The Bloody Tower earned its grim name after King Edward IV's two sons disappeared there in 1483. Many suspect the boys were murdered by their uncle, Richard, so he could steal the throne. The skeletons of two young boys were discovered under a Tower staircase nearly 200 years later.

THE HEADLESS QUEEN

HAUNT SPOT: Chapel of St. Peter ad Vincula

Description: For centuries, castle guards have reported seeing a hooded woman veiled in mist wandering the castle. When she turns to face the guards, her hood is missing a head!

Historical origin: Queen Anne Boleyn, the second wife of King Henry VIII, was unfairly convicted of treason in 1536. Her punishment was swift and brutal: She lost her head.

HIS ROYAL GHOSTLINESS

HAUNT SPOT: Wakefield Tower

Description: Each May 21, as the hour grows late, the ghostly form of King Henry VI is said to stroll through Wakefield Tower, only to disappear at the stroke of midnight.

Historical origin: The king died while imprisoned in this tower on May 21, 1471. Historians suspect he was murdered by a rival for the throne.

THE GRIZZLY SPIRIT

HAUNT SPOT: Martin Tower

Description: A spectral bear materialized before a guard walking the walls, startling him so badly that he died of fright!

Historical origin: The Tower's royal residents kept a menagerie of wild animals, including a grizzly and a polar bear. Perhaps one got loose . . . or maybe a spirit still lumbers through the halls.

AGENT JEEPER'S REALITY CHECK

Researchers estimate that more than 107 billion people lived and died on Earth before you were born, which means the past's dead outnumber today's living by fifteen to one. If ghosts were real, you'd have enough specters hovering nearby to form a basketball team!

TOY OF
TERROR

THIS HAUNTED DOLL PLAYS FOR CREEPS

Robert the doll bides his time in a Key West museum, where he's said to short-circuit the cameras of patrons who snap his picture without first asking permission.

WHEN YOUNG ROBERT EUGENE OTTO ("GENE" TO HIS FRIENDS) GOT IN TROUBLE FOR A MESSY ROOM, BUSTED DISH, OR OTHER HOUSEHOLD MISHAP, HE ALWAYS OFFERED UP THE SAME EXCUSE: "ROBERT DID IT!" But Robert wasn't a roughhousing brother or a precocious pet. He's a doll—3 feet (.9 m) tall with coal-black eyes. And Gene's parents knew their son was telling the truth.

The story goes that Gene received the doll as a gift in 1904 from a maid who worked for the Ottos at their home in Key West, Florida, U.S.A. She did not like Gene's parents, and as revenge she placed a voodoo curse on the doll, giving it a mischievous life of its own. Gene named the doll "Robert," after himself, and the two went everywhere together. Soon, creepy things were afoot in the Otto household.

Gene's parents would overhear their son chatting with the doll in his room, and Robert the doll would answer in a different voice— sometimes with a creepy giggle. The boy and his toy often argued. Alarmed by the racket, Gene's parents would wrench open the bedroom door to find their son cowering before the doll, everything in the room topsy-turvy. "Robert did it!" their son exclaimed.

The boy grew up to become a famous artist, but he still maintained a strange obsession with the doll. He kept Robert in an upstairs room of his parents' house, which he inherited after they passed away. Schoolchildren walking along the sidewalk claimed they saw the doll slinking from window to window. Dinner guests would hear Robert's chilling giggle. If anyone asked about the strange banging and creaking upstairs, Gene would deliver the old excuse: "Robert did it!"

The artist passed away long ago, but his toy is still taking the blame for mysterious mischief. If you try to snap a photo of the doll—now an exhibit at the Fort East Martello Museum in Key West—and your camera mysteriously stops working, you know what to say: "Robert did it."

ETHEL THE E.T.'S
DISTURBING DATA

You think a haunted toy is creepy? What about a haunted toy store? For decades, employees at a Toys "R" Us in Sunnyvale, California, U.S.A., have reported run-ins with a friendly ghost who plays with the toys at night but doesn't put them away.

HAUNTED
HOLIDAYS

SAMHAIN: Two millennia ago, Europe's Celtic people donned costumes every October 31st to honor the dead and ward off evil spirits. Sound like a familiar custom? The festival of Samhain evolved into today's most horribly fun holiday: Halloween.

FRIDAY THE 13TH: Combine the unluckiest day of the week (according to Christianity, for instance, Jesus was crucified on a Friday) with a number associated with evil since the days of the Vikings (even today, most high-rises lack a 13th floor), and you have a disturbing day and date that inspires "paraskevidekatriaphobia," or fear of Friday the 13th. The superstitious call in sick for work and lay low.

HUNGRY GHOST FESTIVAL: When the doors to the spirit realm swing open during the seventh lunar month, according to Chinese tradition, deceased ancestors spill out to mingle with the living. Holiday observers appease restless ghosts by burning incense and leaving out piles of sweets and snacks. Help yourself to the treats and you risk a haunting!

Horrible
HAUNTINGS

"Skeletor" — **AIIIIEEEE!**

Robert the Doll — **TERRIFYING**

Demon Cat — **SPINE-TINGLING**

Queen Anne Boleyn

Brown Lady of Raynham Hall — **UNSETTLING**

CIA

PhEAR FACTOR

PHENOMENA ELICITING ABNORMAL REACTIONS

Agent Jeeper Ranks **FEARSOME PHANTOMS.**

CHAPTER **6**

Creepy
Cosmos

LOOK, UP IN THE SKY! IT'S A BIRD! IT'S A PLANE! IT'S...IT'S...WHAT IN THE WORLD IS THAT?! You've probably asked

that question while squinting at some glowing speck or oddball aircraft hovering in the heavens. If you've spotted something soaring and didn't know what it was, then congrats! You've seen an unidentified flying object, or UFO. Now, whether that streaking smudge was actually an alien spaceship is a question for the UFOlogists, or people who study mysterious objects in the sky. You'll become a UFOlogist yourself by the time you finish this chapter on alien visitors, flying saucers, and the search for life out there.

SPACE INVA

400

ART FOR ALIENS
The people of Peru's ancient Nazca culture trace titanic animals, rectangles the length of landing strips, and abstract shapes larger than football fields on the floor of a desert plateau. The figures only make sense when seen from above—some even look like modern-day runways—leading UFOlogists to believe they were created for alien visitors.

1896

ATTACK OF THE AIRSHIP
Newspapers from California to Illinois begin citing eyewitness reports of a mysterious airship. Thousands of Americans claim to see the craft, described as cigar-shaped with propellers and wings. Such "heavier-than-air" vehicles hadn't been invented yet.

1992

EARTH'S TWIN
Astronomers detect the first exoplanets—worlds orbiting distant stars outside our solar system. More than a thousand have been discovered since, although scientists are still on the lookout for Earth-like planets in "Goldilocks Zones"—orbital regions that are neither too hot nor too cold, but just right to support life.

1960

THE SEARCH BEGINS
Scientists begin scanning the universe with special telescopes for radio signals from alien civilizations. The project is called SETI, or the Search for Extraterrestrial Intelligence. It hasn't picked up any alien broadcasts yet, but the scientists are still listening.

DERS

JUNE 1947

1944

FLYING SAUCER MARK 1
While flying near Washington's Mt. Rainer, pilot Kenneth Arnold spots several unidentified objects skipping through the sky. From his description of the craft as saucer-like, the press invents the term "flying saucer." Sightings of similar craft begin popping up across the United States.

FOO'D YOU
Fighter pilots in World War II report seeing balls of fire chasing their aircraft and skimming along the ground. Believing these strange lights are some new type of weapon, the pilots name them "foo fighters."

JUNE 1947

1953

THE ROSWELL INCIDENT
A flying object hits the dirt near the small town of Roswell, New Mexico. Air Force officials insist it's just a weather balloon, but conspiracy theorists later accuse the U.S. government of hushing up a UFO crash. The Roswell saga becomes central to UFOlogy. Turn the page to read what really happened.

PROJECT BLUEBOOK
The U.S. Air Force ramps up a program to study sightings of UFOs (a term coined that same year). By 1969, when "Project Bluebook" ends, the Air Force will have investigated nearly 13,000 eyewitness reports. Today, 701 of those sightings remain unexplained.

Crash Course

What Went Down at Roswell

A WRECKED SPACESHIP. ALIEN BODIES PULLED FROM THE WRECKAGE. GOVERNMENT AGENTS DISPATCHED TO COVER UP THE EVIDENCE. Even if you can't pinpoint the town of Roswell on a New Mexico, U.S.A., map, you might've heard the details of its famous 1947 "incident." Or at least you think you've heard the details, which have been distorted by conspiracy theorists and Hollywood storytellers. For the real story, we need to separate fact from science fiction.

Yes, a UFO did crash outside the town of Roswell in the summer of 1947. A rancher named William "Mac" Brazel discovered the wreckage. Linking it to a recent rash of flying-saucer sightings, Brazel reported the debris to the sheriff, who in turn called the nearby Roswell Army Air Field (RAAF). After investigating the wreckage, Army officials issued a press release saying they've recovered a "flying disk."

That doozy of an announcement led to a startling headline in the local paper: "RAAF Captures Flying Saucer on Ranch in Roswell Region." According to the story, residents spotted a glowing object in the sky before the crash, and military officials confiscated the wreckage. As newspapers across the country began reporting on the Roswell incident, military officials quickly changed their story. The Roswell debris wasn't a flying disk after all, they said. It was a high-altitude balloon used to study the weather. The explanation fit with Brazel's description of the debris: bits of rubber, tinfoil, some sticks, and tough paper. Case closed; end of story. The Roswell incident was quietly forgotten for the next 30 years.

REVISITING ROSWELL: THE GREAT DEBATE

ETHEL THE E.T.'S TAKE...

Whoa, whoa, whoa—the Roswell case isn't even close to closed! What about all the eyewitnesses who came forward in the 1970s with crashed-saucer stories? Some claimed they saw tiny alien corpses recovered from the wreckage, spirited away to military bases for secret experiments. Others insisted the debris contained impossibly strong metal alloys not of this world. At least one former Air Force officer swore there was not one, but two crashes. The conspiracy grew deeper—and creepier—with each new witness!

AGENT JEEPER'S TAKE...

Oh, relax. The U.S. government released a report in the mid-1990s that put all those kooky conspiracies to rest. It revealed that the 1947 debris was actually a crashed balloon in its top-secret Project Mogul, which used high-altitude sensors to monitor for enemy nuclear-missile tests. And those supposed alien corpses? They were crash-test dummies dropped from miles in the sky to check parachute technology. A lot of these events happened after 1947. Your "eyewitnesses" got them all mixed up with the Roswell crash, and the tale grew with the telling.

UFOs

THE FIRST UFO

A mysterious shape swoops across a cloudscape near Mt. Washington, New Hampshire, U.S.A., in this photo from 1870. Looks like a blimp, right? Except that such airships were a rarity at this point in history.

THE BARNSTORMER

A married couple spotted this saucer-shaped disk soaring toward their farm from the distant mountains near McMinnville, Oregon, U.S.A., in 1950. The husband rushed from the house to snap two pictures—among the most famous ever taken of a UFO.

A CLOSE-UP LOOK AT
Close Encounters...

BELGIUM'S UFO BOOM

Thousands of eyewitnesses spotted strange triangular objects flying over Belgium in 1989 and 1990. The nation's air force even scrambled fighter jets to chase one mysterious craft. Skeptics suspect the UFOs were helicopters or perhaps experimental American stealth planes in Belgian airspace.

VOLCANIC PANIC

Footage aired on a Mexican television station in October 2012 showed a sleek cylindrical shape dive-bomb into the crater of a volcano near Mexico City, a hot spot of UFO activity for decades.

SCENIC SAUCER

The woman who snapped this photo in 1981 thought she was just taking a pretty picture of a mountain on Vancouver Island, Canada. Imagine her surprise after she developed the photo and noticed the creepy disk-shaped UFO hovering in the sky!

FLUORESCENT FLIER

Eyewitnesses across eastern Kentucky reported seeing a shimmering shape hovering high in the sky for more than two hours in October 2012. Some speculate it was a weather balloon or even a toy airship that got loose from its owner.

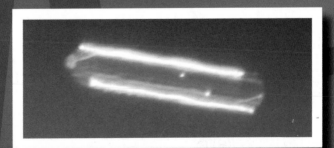

No.

NAME **CRP005**

Creepy Case File #5: Unidentified Sunken Object

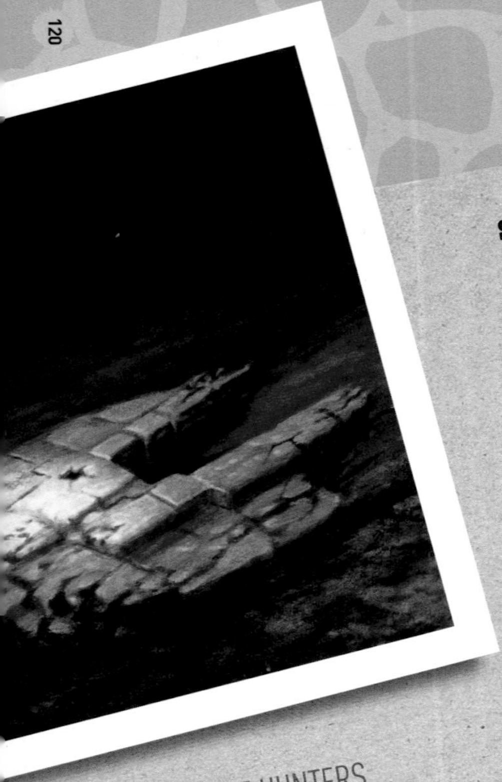

SUBJECT: The "Baltic Sea Anomaly," an underwater formation shaped like a spaceship

LOCATION: The Baltic Sea

TIME FRAME: A.D. 2011 to present

CASE BACKGROUND:

They were searching for sunken ships, but the Swedish deep-sea salvage team known as Ocean X found something else entirely. Scanning the bottom of the Baltic Sea with as sonar—a sensor that uses sound waves to detect images underwater—the team discovered an odd circular structure roughly 200 feet (60 m) across at a depth of 300 feet (90 m). It was sitting at the end of a long gouge in the silt, as if it had skidded to a halt. Had the object crash-landed here?

Ocean X's team members were intrigued. They publicized their fuzzy sonar image of the object, which came to be known as the Baltic Sea Anomaly. Observers across the Internet noticed its uncanny resemblance to the Millennium Falcon from the Star Wars films. Some speculated that it was a crashed flying saucer, or perhaps an old anti-submarine installation, or maybe even an underwater gateway to another world. Ocean X's members thought the Anomaly could be the undersea equivalent of England's mysterious Stonehenge rock circle. Whatever it was, the structure was getting a lot of attention.

DID TREASURE HUNTERS
DISCOVER A UFO
AT THE BOTTOM OF THE
BALTIC SEA?

CASE ANALYSIS:

In spite of mysterious equipment failures (cameras and other electronics reportedly quit working when carried close to the Anomaly), Ocean X's divers and robotic submarines managed to gather samples of the structure. Scientific analysis of those samples hasn't revealed anything out of this world yet. Instead of exotic alien metals or man-made materials, the Anomaly appears to be made of ordinary rocks, likely deposited ages ago when glaciers crept across what is now the Baltic Sea's bottom.

Still, the Ocean X team isn't giving up on their studies or their quest to focus their studies on strange lines on the Anomaly's surface and a mysterious black attention-grabbing discovery. They plan to find any evidence of extraterrestrial material. Who knows if they'll learn more about Earth in the process. life, but perhaps they'll learn more about Earth in the process.

ETHEL THE E.T.'S
DISTURBING DATA

Space stinks. No joke! Astronauts returning from space walks claim their suits have a metallic odor similar to welding fumes. Now you know why I never open the window of my saucer.

Tales of HELPLESS HUMANS taken for a ride

Abduc

One minute, you're hiking through the forest, riding in a car, or maybe just chilling in front of the TV. The next, you wake up somewhere else—and with hours missing from your memory. Then the nightmares begin.

So goes the typical chain of events of a close encounter of the fourth kind, also known as an alien abduction. Thousands of people claim they've lived through such a creepy experience: beamed aboard an extraterrestrial spaceship, only to be prodded, probed, and perhaps even implanted with alien doodads. Tagged and returned to Earth, the abductees typically have no recollection of their

Those memories come later, in the form of scary dreams and flashbacks. Because abductees usually lack physical evidence of their ordeals, they're often met with disbelief. Most scientists believe alien-abduction stories are flights of fantasy—figments of the imagination or a sort of self-hypnosis. Another culprit could be sleep paralysis, a disorder that brings about vivid dreams of being held down and inspected by shadowy figures. Nevertheless, some abductees have passed lie-detector tests when quizzed about their experiences. You might not believe their terrifying tales, but they

UP AND AWAY:
THE FIRST FAMOUS ABDUCTION

Betty and Barney Hill were driving home on a New Hampshire, U.S.A., road in 1961 when they noticed they were being followed—by a star! The couple stopped their car and stared in awe as the glowing object resolved into a cylindrical-shaped spacecraft. Barney noticed inhuman faces peering from its portholes. The next thing the couple knew, they were 35 miles (56 km) farther down the road. Two hours had mysteriously elapsed, but they couldn't remember a thing. Later, the Hills began to recall scary details, such as being led into the spaceship, stuck with needles, and having samples scraped from their skin. Theirs was the first widely known case of alien abduction. The state of New Hampshire even commemorated their experience with a roadside plaque at the spot where they were taken. Dare you drive by it on a starry night?

BETTY AND BARNEY HILL
INCIDENT

On the night of September 19-20, 1961, Portsmouth, NH couple Betty and Barney Hill experienced a close encounter with an unidentified flying object and two hours of "lost" time while driving south on Rte 3 near Lincoln. They filed an official Air Force Project Blue Book report of a brightly-lit cigar-shaped craft the next day, but were not public with their story until it was leaked

ted!

The second kind:
Observing a UFO and its effects (wind, heat, etc.)

The first kind:
Seeing a UFO

The third kind:
Seeing the UFO's crew

The seventh kind:
Starting a family with an alien

The MANY Kinds
of CLOSE
ENCOUNTERS...

The fourth kind:
Being abducted by a UFO or its crew

The sixth kind:
Being killed by a UFO or its occupants

The fifth kind:
Making voluntary contact with a UFO or its crew

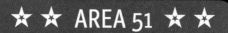

★ ★ **AREA 51** ★ ★

SPOOKY
SPOT

Fly high above the desert of southern Nevada, U.S.A., and you might spot a mysterious airbase in the middle of nowhere. Notice any UFOs sticking out of the hangars down there? Spot any little green men hunkered in the bunkers? This miles-high perspective is the closest you will get to Area 51, the super-top-secret military facility located far from snooping civilians. (Even its airspace is restricted, so don't dawdle!) Established in 1955, Area 51 is the government's testing ground for classified craft. Conspiracy theorists suspect it's home to something creepier: alien technology. Could they be on to something? The truth is down there . . .

ROAD TO NOWHERE: Nevada officially designated this nearby stretch of State Route 375 as the "Extraterrestrial Highway" after so many motorists reported UFO sightings in Area 51's airspace. Were drivers spotting experimental airplanes . . . or flying saucers commandeered by Area 51's test pilots?

SIGNS OF TROUBLE: Head down the dirt road leading to Area 51's front gate and you'll get the feeling you're not exactly welcome here. Guards won't pounce from behind the cacti to shout "halt," but their scary signs speak louder than words. Area 51 is not only off-limits, the government insists it doesn't exist!

LANDING ZONE: With its miles of runways and protected airspace, Area 51 is the perfect proving ground for experimental spy planes and remote-control drones. Conspiracy theorists think those landing strips—one is nearly 5 miles (8 km) long—are ideal for something else: testing vehicles "reverse-engineered" from recovered alien technology.

UFO STORAGE: More than two dozen hangars dot the base. Whatever lies inside is classified, but UFOlogists have long suspected the government of storing the crashed Roswell UFO somewhere in Area 51. The bodies of the alien pilots are supposedly here, too, presumably kept on ice underground.

AGENT JEEPER'S
REALITY CHECK

If Area 51 does really exist—and I'm not saying it does—the only "alien" technology tested here was a fighter jet recovered from the former Soviet Union. But you didn't hear that from me!

MARTIAN

MARTIAN SAUCERS

THE "PROOF": One eagle-eyed observer noted something curious in footage transmitted by the Mars rover Curiosity just days after it landed in 2012. Four sphere-shaped ships appear to hover in the pink-tinged sky. Could they be flying saucers in the Martian air force? Or visitors from another planet?

THE TRUTH: Image experts say the unidentified flying objects are neither flying nor objects. They're simply visual glitches in the rover's imaging system.

SPACE FACE

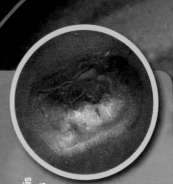

THE "PROOF": When the Viking 1 orbiter snapped this photo of Mars in 1976, it became a sensation for its apparent portrayal of a mountainous Martian face resembling an Egyptian pharaoh.

THE TRUTH: Eager to set the record straight on this crowd-pleasing Mars anomaly, NASA used a satellite to rephotograph the region in 1998 and 2001. The high-resolution retakes revealed a natural geological feature rather than a monument to Martiankind.

FREAKY FORESTS

THE "PROOF": If Mars is such a lifeless lump of rock, then what's with these eerie trees sprouting among the red dunes? And where there's a Martian forest, there must be Martian wildlife, right?

THE TRUTH: Your Earthling eyes are playing tricks on you. These "trees" are actually streaks of sediment blasted aloft by geysers of evaporating carbon dioxide. The sediment settles on the ground downwind of the dunes, creating streak patterns.

MADNESS!

SPOOKY "PROOF" OF LIFE ON THE RED PLANET...OR NOT

Astronomers peering at Mars in the 17th and 18th centuries saw signs of life everywhere. Seas! Continents! Canals for Martian shipping! But modern telescopes, orbital probes, and NASA landers ruined the fun by revealing our planetary neighbor's dry details: It's just a lifeless ball of red rock and sand dunes. As robotic rovers continue to scour the Martian landscape for signs that life once existed on the red planet, Earthling alien hunters claim the proof is already out there, plain to see in these images beamed from the fourth rock from the sun . . .

ETHEL THE E.T.'S
DISTURBING DATA

Radio listeners who tuned in late to a 1938 Halloween broadcast of H. G. Wells's science-fiction book *War of the Worlds* experienced a different kind of Mars madness. They thought the program was a genuine news report of a Martian invasion! Good thing I didn't swing by Earth for some Halloween candy in 1938!

BIGFOOT THE EXTRATERRESTRIAL

THE "PROOF": Mars enthusiasts studying panoramic pictures from NASA's Spirit rover made a chilling discovery when they zoomed in on this particular photo, which seems to show a humanoid Martian out for an afternoon strut. The figure has been likened to everything from Sasquatch to a *Star Wars* Tusken Raider.

THE TRUTH: Scrutiny of the strolling humanoid reveals that it's only a few feet from the rover, which means the Martian Bigfoot is either itty-bitty or just an oddly shaped rock.

Creepy Case File #6: The Blob From Above

SUBJECT: "Star jelly," a gross goo thought to fall from space

LOCATION: Worldwide

TIME FRAME: Medieval times to present

CASE BACKGROUND:

In the 1958 monster-movie classic *The Blob*, an alien amoeba crash-lands on Earth and begins gobbling up everything—and everyone—in its path, growing as it goes. The film was creepier: The film was everyone—in its path, growing as it goes. Creepy? Yes. Even creepier: The film was inspired by true events!

Eight years earlier, two Philadelphia, U.S.A., policemen patrolling at night witnessed a UFO of a different sort: an unidentified falling object. When they crept to the object's landing spot in a nearby field, they discovered a glob of jelly 6 feet (1.8 m) wide giving off a purplish glow. Then one of the officers did something that defied common sense: He reached out and touched the goo. It melted under his fingertips, leaving behind a sticky residue. Within 20 minutes, the glob had dissolved completely.

Similar accounts of so-called star jelly discoveries go back to medieval times. The slimy substance comes in many shapes and sizes—all of them icky, semitransparent, and said to smell like sulfur (a rotten-egg odor associated with meteorites). Accounts are often associated with the goo's meteor showers, which explains the goo's alternate names "star rot" and "star spawn." Scientists have studied star jelly to see if it's really from outer space, and whether this cosmic mucus might have served as the origin of life on Earth.

IS ALIEN SLIME HITCHHIKING TO EARTH ON METEORS?

CASE ANALYSIS:

A storm of goo drenched a small town in Washington, U.S.A., in 1994 after an annual meteor shower. More recently, odd blobs have been popping up in the Scottish countryside. Scientists have managed to gather the goo before it dissolved, but none of their probing has proven that it's of extraterrestrial origin.

In fact, the explanations are disappointingly down to Earth. Some samples turned out to be a type of algae that swells in size after rainstorms. In other cases, star jelly is slime mold: a fungus-like life-form that creeps across the forest floor on the hunt for bacteria. Some jellies were actually bits of frog upchucked by other animals. The truth is, lots of organic and artificial substances—from soaring spores to slush leaked from airplane toilets—fit the description of star jelly.

But if you'd rather believe the Blob really exists somewhere up there, consider these two unsettling facts: Studies have shown that organic goo can survive a meteorite crash, and scientists in India are convinced that a slimy storm of bloodred rain in 2001 was not of this Earth.

Star jelly: slime from outer space or bird barf? The truth is grosser than fiction.

129

HOLY SMOKE: A saucer-like craft appears ready to beam up the central figures in this work depicting the baptism of Jesus Christ, painted 300 years ago.

ODD BALL: A man in the background of this 15th-century painting peers skyward as if to say, "What the heck is that spiky ball up there?!"

SAUCER SWARM: An apparent fleet of flying saucers descends on Rome in this painting from the early 1400s.

Spacing OUT

PhEAR FACTOR

PHENOMENA ELICITING ABNORMAL REACTIONS

Ethel the E.T. Ranks **ALIEN ODDITIES.**

AIIIIEEEE!	Close Encounters of the Fourth Kind
TERRIFYING	Roswell Incident
SPINE-TINGLING	Area 51
UNSETTLING	Star Jelly

131

CHAPTER **7**

The Fringe

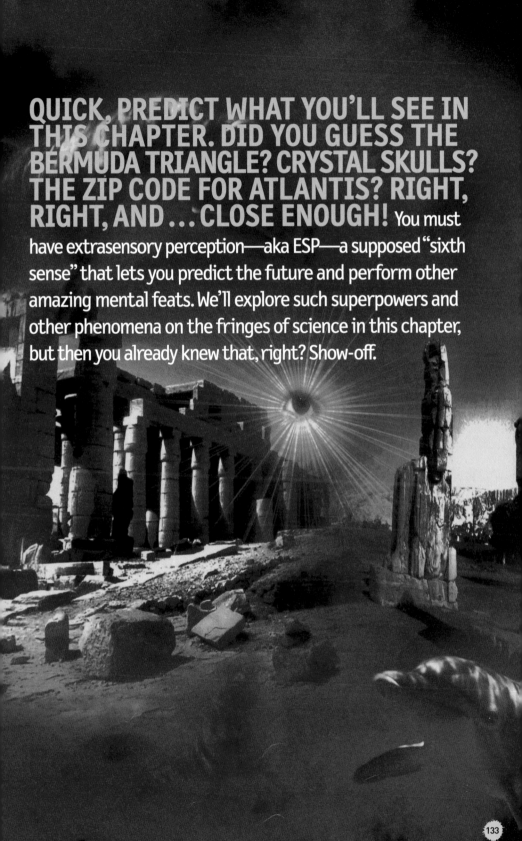

QUICK, PREDICT WHAT YOU'LL SEE IN THIS CHAPTER. DID YOU GUESS THE BERMUDA TRIANGLE? CRYSTAL SKULLS? THE ZIP CODE FOR ATLANTIS? RIGHT, RIGHT, AND … CLOSE ENOUGH! You must have extrasensory perception—aka ESP—a supposed "sixth sense" that lets you predict the future and perform other amazing mental feats. We'll explore such superpowers and other phenomena on the fringes of science in this chapter, but then you already knew that, right? Show-off.

YOUR MIND IS BURSTING WITH AMAZING ABILITIES, FROM SOLVING STICKY ALGEBRA PROBLEMS TO OUTWITTING THE FINAL BOSS IN *SUPER MARIO BROS.* But have you ever had a dream that came true? Or a gut feeling that saved your butt? Researchers who study "parapsychology" label these momentous mental moments as examples of extrasensory perception (ESP)—senses that don't rely on sight, smell, hearing, touch, or taste. Feast your mind's eye on these four famous examples . . .

thinking BIG

CLAIRVOYANCE

A combination of the French words for "clear" and "vision," clairvoyance is the ability to mentally visualize people, objects, or events that are somewhere else—even on the other side of the world! With a power like that, who needs cable TV?

MOST CONVINCING CASE: **As part of its top-secret Stargate Project, the United States government recruited psychic spies with "remote-viewing" powers for mental missions, such as peeking at military bases in other countries and assisting with hostage rescues. The program was shut down in 1995, despite some promising results in the laboratory.**

TELEPATHY

Think of this power as a cell phone inside your skull: the ability to receive the thoughts of others and send mental messages in return. Parapsychologists believe these messages are transmitted as electromagnetic energy or perhaps a type of "brain wave" that has yet to be discovered.

MOST CONVINCING CASE: **In the late 1930s, an author in New York and an explorer in the Arctic put their heads together to conduct a five-month experiment in long-distance telepathy. Each day, the two men transmitted mental images to each other, then recorded the results in a diary. When they got together later to compare notes, the men found a surprising number of instances where their minds seemed in sync.**

TELEKINESIS

More like extrasensory projection than perception, telekinesis is the flexing of mental muscles to move objects in the real world. It works like the Force in the *Star Wars* films, when Jedi knights chuck chunks of metal with just a wave of the hand.

MOST CONVINCING CASE: While growing up in the former Soviet Union, a girl named Nina Kulagina noticed things would move when she got mad. After she learned to focus her powers, Soviet officials videotaped her shoving objects on tables and plucking matchsticks from piles of them with her mind. Skeptics think she faked these feats through magician's sleight of hand.

PRECOGNITION

Perhaps the eeriest of the ESP powers, precognition is the ability to foresee the future. Conveniently enough, skeptics claim, such foresight often takes the form of cryptic images and mysterious visions that only seem to foretell events after the fact.

MOST CONVINCING CASE: In Morgan Robertson's short story "Futility," a supposedly unsinkable ship called the *Titan* strikes an iceberg in mid-April and goes under. Many passengers die because the ship doesn't carry enough lifeboats. Sounds like a story about the *Titanic*, right? There's just one thing: "Futility" was written 14 years before the *Titanic* hit an iceberg and sunk in mid-April 1912.

FOUR SUPPOSED SUPERPOWERS OF THE HUMAN BRAIN

AGENT JEEPER'S REALITY CHECK

I'm not surprised my fellow G-men canceled the Stargate Project. A lot of supposed ESP can be chalked up to coincidence. After all, with seven billion people on Earth, someone somewhere is bound to have a dream or stray thought that seems to match some important event. As for the precognitive powers of the author of "Futility," he was an expert on ships who figured an accident like the *Titanic*'s was bound to happen.

Creepy Case File #7: Bones of Stone

SUBJECT: The "Skull of Doom" and other similar quartz carvings

LOCATION: Mexico and Central America

TIME FRAME: 1700 B.C. to A.D. 1930

CASE BACKGROUND:

They are believed to have the powers to heal and kill, transmit psychic messages, and portend the end of the world. Crystal skulls are among archaeology's most controversial and creepy artifacts. A dozen or so of these quartz sculptures—some crystal clear, and others milky white—sit in private and public collections around the world, and they range in size from 15 inches (38 cm) high to itty-bitty. Even the small skulls project an air of scary mystery.

Crystal skulls began appearing in museums in the 1860s, allegedly recovered from Mexico and Central America and once used in bloody rituals of the ancient Aztec and Maya. Some claim the skulls were artifacts from the lost land of Atlantis. Others believe they were alien gadgets given to the Aztec for unimaginable purposes. Spiritualists covet each skull as a sort of otherworldly powers.

Frederick A. Mitchell-Hedges, a of Swiss Army knife explorer and author of slick-talking 1930s astounding tales, claims he found the most famous crystal skull of all while searching for a lost Maya civilization in Central America. According to Mitchell-Hedges, the human-size skull was crafted at least 3,600 years ago, painstakingly hand-polished for generations from a solid block of crystal. It was "the embodiment of all evil," Mitchell-Hedges wrote. "Several people who have cynically laughed at it have died." His find became known as the "Skull of Doom."

ARE CRYSTAL SKULLS OR AN SUPERNATURAL RELICS ELABORATE HOAX?

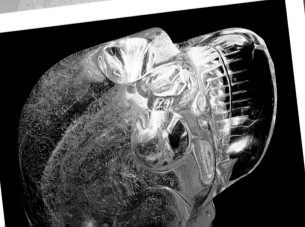

The Skull of Doom's owner wrote that it was "used by the high priest of the Maya. When he willed death with the help of the skull, death invariably followed."

Microscopic study of the skulls shows they were carved with relatively modern tools and techniques.

Facial reconstruction of the Skull of Doom revealed the features of a modern European woman rather than a Mesoamerican from 3,600 years ago.

High-tech sensors detected no out-of-this-world activity in one crystal skull.

CASE ANALYSIS:

Crystal skulls have a fishy history. Many are linked to a French antiquities dealer who peddled them to museums in the 1800s, when interest in ancient cultures was at an all-time high. Yet none of these stone bones have turned up at official excavation sites, nor do they bear the traits of authentic Central American artifacts.

Nevertheless, as long as historians couldn't disprove their ancient origins, the skulls lured legions of true believers. That changed recently. Scrutiny under modern electron microscopes revealed that the skulls were made in the mid- to late 1800s—at just the right time for a certain French dealer to cash in on the artifacts craze. The notorious Skull of Doom is a more recent creation, likely from the 20th century. Still, stories of its powers persist. (It shoots lasers from its eyes! It can make hard drives crash!) Laugh at the tales if you dare.

137

Poltergeists

WHEN THE PARANORMAL GETS PUSHY ...

Ghosts may rattle dishes, materialize as spooky apparitions, and generally scare people witless, but they never harm the living—or so paranormal investigators believe. The same can't be said of a different class of unruly entities known as poltergeists. These freaky forces allegedly rearrange furniture, slam doors, and even bite humans. Above all, poltergeists make a racket!

In fact, the word "poltergeist" means "noisy ghost" in German. Yet paranormal experts believe poltergeists aren't ghosts at all. (That is to say, they're not restless spirits of the dearly departed.) Instead, poltergeists are thought to be the product of living humans—neighbors, kid sisters, and sometimes even the very people under attack.

How is that possible? Blame telekinesis: the power to move matter with the mind. Paranormal investigators believe poltergeists are caused by accidental outbursts of this mental ability. Imagine if you possessed telekinesis but didn't know it. Any temper tantrum could send furniture flying across the neighbor's living room or spill dishes from the kitchen cabinets. Suddenly, your neighborhood is under assault from a "noisy ghost"— one that you've unwittingly unleashed with your own noggin! What's worse: Paranormal experts believe poltergeists can take on a life of their own to terrify victims with growls and creepy voices.

THE **BELL** WITCH
A PROMINENT POLTERGEIST

Pioneer John Bell thought he'd found the perfect spot to settle when he built a house on the Tennessee, U.S.A., frontier in the early 1800s. But soon an unseen force began tormenting Bell's daughter Betsy, tugging her hair and scratching her skin. Terrified, the family enlisted help from neighbors, who came from miles around to witness furniture crashing and other unseen effects of the "Bell Witch." Even former president Andrew Jackson was said to pay a visit—only to beat a hasty retreat when his coach's wheels mysteriously locked. The Bell Witch went quiet after John Bell's death, although tourists insist that things are amiss in a creepy cave near the house . . .

ENTITY
IDENTIFICATION

	Poltergeist	Ghost
MOVES OBJECTS:	💀	💀
MAKES NOISE:	💀	💀
SMASHES THINGS:	💀	
TALKS TO THE LIVING:	💀	💀
OCCASIONALLY VISIBLE:		💀
ATTACKS PEOPLE:	💀	

What on Earth?

FIVE CASES OF NATURE ACTING STRANGER...

UPSIDE-DOWN HILLS

The old adage "What goes up must come down" doesn't apply on "gravity hills," topsy-turvy outdoor oddities found in more than 20 states and all over the world. Also known as mystery hills and magnetic hills, gravity hills look like any stretch of hilly road until you let a ball loose on the asphalt. Instead of rolling downhill, the ball rolls upward, as if pulled by some mysterious force.

WHAT'S GOING ON? **Pupils of the paranormal may blame gravity hills on crashed UFOs or magnetic meteorites, but the truth is more down to Earth. All such hills are actually optical illusions caused when background terrain makes a gentle downhill slope look as if it's actually leaning uphill. Cars that appear to roll uphill are actually going downhill, and the law of gravity remains unbroken.**

GREAT BALLS OF FIRE

It comes into the world as a sizzling ball of energy roughly the size of a human noggin. It makes its grand exit with a small explosion. Ball lightning is one of nature's freakiest special effects, an orb of fire that dances over the ground and launches high into the sky. It's no wonder that eyewitnesses have confused these electrical spheres for everything from galloping ghosts to flying saucers.

WHAT'S GOING ON? **Scientists have concocted all sorts of origin stories for this elusive phenomenon. Some suspect that ball lightning sparks to life when normal lightning strikes the ground and ignites silicon, a chemical element in the soil. The silicon erupts in a fiery globe of burning oxygen that darts willy-nilly through the air.**

STREAKING STONES

Not much moves in California's Death Valley, a seared landscape of sand dunes and dry mud subjected to daily extremes of heat and cold. But strange things are stirring in a lake bed called the "Racetrack." Rocks that tumble to the valley floor have a habit of hiking across the cracked ground, some as far as 1,500 feet (457 m), leaving crooked trails during their travels. Stranger still, no one has actually witnessed the stones in motion.

WHAT'S GOING ON? **Scientists still aren't certain what's animating these inanimate objects. Studies have ruled out earthquakes and gravity (some rocks travel uphill). One theory holds that little donuts of ice form around the stones in the winter, making them float across the flat ground. Other scientists suspect that gusting wind moves the rocks after rains slicken the lake bed.**

ROADSIDE AURORA

Travel nine miles (14 km) east of Marfa, Texas, U.S.A., on Highway 90 and you'll find a parking lot appointed with tables overlooking lackluster scrubland. It seems like a pitiful spot for a picnic during the day, so what draws people here as the sun sets behind the Chinati Mountains? There, in the distance! Twinkling balls of red, white, and blue light seem to float above the ground. They collide, split apart, and dance across the desert. Known as the Marfa Lights, these rarely seen sparkles have been putting on a show for at least a hundred years.

WHAT'S GOING ON? Popular tales link the lights to Native American spirits and the ghosts of gold prospectors, but skeptics think there's a perfectly natural explanation. Scientists suspect the orbs are simply the distant reflections of car headlights or a type of atmospheric mirage.

TOAD STORM

Think the patter of raindrops on your roof is a soothing sound? What about the splatter of falling amphibians? Residents in a Serbian town scrambled for cover in 2005 when thousands of frogs plummeted from above. What's more, such storms have happened before. Deluges of frogs, fish, squid, shells, and worms have been reported since the days of ancient Rome.

WHAT'S GOING ON? When a tornado passes over a swamp or lake, it sucks up the surface water and anything in it—including frogs and fish. The twister can carry this squishy cargo for several miles until its winds weaken, which results in a hail of aquatic creatures. Creepy? Yes, but at least it's better than raining cats and dogs.

DEEP
TROUBLE

"WE CAN'T TELL WHERE WE ARE," the panicked pilot's voice crackled over the radio. "It looks like we are entering white water . . . We're completely lost." So went the final transmission of Flight 19, a group of five U.S. Navy torpedo bombers that took off on a training mission in 1945 and vanished over the Atlantic Ocean. Search crews found no trace of the planes or the 14 men aboard them. Their disappearance spawned a legend—the legend of the Bermuda Triangle.

A vast region of the Atlantic bounded by Bermuda, Miami, and Puerto Rico, the Bermuda Triangle is notorious for swallowing planes, boats, and ships. Craft go missing without leaving behind a dab of debris—not a rivet or life preserver. Known to some as the "Devil's Triangle," this eerie area is certainly an easy place to get lost . . . or worse. Swift currents and sudden storms send ships swirling in circles. Navigators going back to the days of Christopher Columbus reported confusing compass readings. Pilots have complained of an eerie electrical fog that interferes with their instruments. Shipwrecking

AGENT JEEPER'S
Triangle Theories

IT'S GOT GAS
Methane gas locked in the Bermuda Triangle's sediment might belch loose in a bubble barrage capable of sinking ships and disrupting a plane's instruments. Skeptical scientists point out that these gas pockets exist elsewhere in the ocean and don't result in weird disappearances.

ACCIDENTS HAPPEN
The Bermuda Triangle has been a superhighway for sea traffic since the early days of exploration, so it makes sense that the region would see more accidents than less traveled areas. Wreckage not set adrift by the strong currents could sink into the region's trenches, never to be seen again.

ETHEL THE E.T.'S
Triangle Theories

IT'S A DIMENSIONAL PORTAL
Some believe the Bermuda Triangle is actually a giant doorway to ... somewhere else. Planes and ships go in but they never come out!

ATLANTIS LIES BELOW
When divers discovered the strange undersea rock formation known as Bimini Road in the Bahamas, people wondered if they'd found Atlantis, a legendary island believed to have sunk into the Atlantic Ocean long ago (geologists say no). Some believe ancient Atlantean technology still hums beneath the surface, zapping any ships and planes in range.

reefs lie just under the surface in some places; the seafloor dips into abyssal trenches five miles (8 km) deep in others.

Accurate records of the lost are hard to find. According to one reckoning, 75 planes and hundreds of yachts have gone missing in the Devil's Triangle in the past century. Why is this stretch of turquoise sea such a hot spot for vanishings? We can't ask the long-lost crew members of Flight 19, but the hosts of *That's Creepy!* have their own explanations . . .

No.

NAME: CRP008

Creepy Case File #8: The "Bloop" From Below

SUBJECT: "Bloop," a mysterious deep-ocean sound

LOCATION: Far off the Pacific coast of southern South America.

TIME FRAME: A.D. 1997

CASE BACKGROUND:

The ocean is a noisy place. Whales sing, volcanoes spew, currents surge, icebergs crumble, and glaciers tumble into the sea. Ships and submarines add their background buzz. Using arrays of sensitive underwater microphones called hydrophones, scientists monitor this aquatic racket. They can usually file deep-sea sounds into one of three categories: boat traffic, geological activity, or marine life.

In the summer of 1997, researchers recorded a noise they'd never heard before . . . and it was loud. The signal was detected by Pacific Ocean hydrophones nearly 3,000 miles (4,800 km) apart, making it louder than any known animal noise. Scientists named it "Bloop." They haven't heard it since.

DID RESEARCHERS RECORD A SEA MONSTER'S MOAN?

CASE ANALYSIS:

"We use sound to study phenomena in the global ocean, and we understand most of what we hear," says Christopher Fox, who monitors hydrophones for the U.S. National Oceanic and Atmospheric Administration (NOAA). Bloop wasn't so easy to understand. It warbled from the abyss for a full minute, well, exactly in frequency. Play it in fast forward and it sounds, gradually rising like a bloop! Fox suspects the noise might come from some type of animal. But which animal? Bloop is so overpowering, it could drown out the song of the blue whale, the loudest and largest animal in the ocean. Whatever made Bloop might be even larger—a true monster of the deep. For now, NOAA will only classify Bloop's origin as unknown. "There are unusual sounds in the ocean that we do not understand, coming from unknown sources," Fox says, "and that's creepy."

WHAT'S BEHIND BLOOP?

A **marine mammal?** Nope. Bloop is much louder than the loudest whale.

A **giant squid?** Doubtful. The "Kraken" lacks the organs to create such a racket.

An **undersea volcano?** Unlikely. Bloop falls outside the range of sounds created by geological activity.

An **undiscovered sea monster?** Possibly! Scientists know more about the surface of the moon than the depths of the ocean. A big beast could very well lurk below . . .

HOAXES IN THE
HEADLINES

Bigfoot's
BODY
FOUND!

After claiming they discovered a Sasquatch carcass in the Georgia, U.S.A., wilderness in 2008, two hunters put the body on ice and submitted it for scientific study.

Turns out the **"BODY"** was just a rubber gorilla costume, and supposed Sasquatch tissue samples were actually from a possum. *Oh, and the hunters just happened to co-own a company that offered Bigfoot tours.*

LOCH NESS MONSTER SIGHTED!

The slender neck of "Nessie" pokes from Loch Ness in this famous 1934 picture, the longest-standing piece of photographic proof that a serpent lurks in the lake. A person involved with the picture admitted in 1994 that it was a hoax. Nessie's neck, he claimed, is just a plastic model glued to a tin toy submarine.

MERMAID MUMMY DISCOVERED!

Circus showman P. T. Barnum displayed the long-dead body of a so-called Fiji Mermaid in the 1800s. Such mummified mermaids were once common curiosities, but they were nothing more than creepy craft projects made from stitched-together animal parts and paper-mâché.

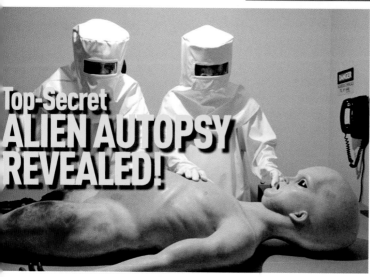

Top-Secret ALIEN AUTOPSY REVEALED!

A ratings sensation when it aired on television in 1995, this grainy black-and-white film supposedly showed scientists slicing open a dead extraterrestrial and plucking out its organs. The film's producer claimed he obtained the footage from a secret military contact involved with the 1947 UFO crash near Roswell, New Mexico, but he later admitted the footage was fabricated.

UFOs Make Their Mark!

When intricate swirls started appearing in English cornfields in the 1970s, believers in the paranormal hailed them as evidence of artistic visitors from . . . somewhere else. (Hint: Look up.) Crop-circle fever gripped the nation—until two pranksters admitted they used ropes and boards to press the mysterious designs into the fields.

FLIGHT OF THE MOTHMAN

Did this SPOOKY CREATURE terrorize a West Virginia town?

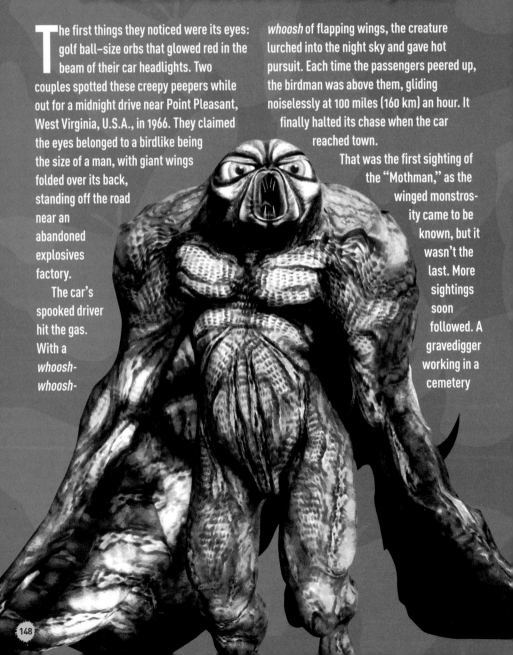

The first things they noticed were its eyes: golf ball–size orbs that glowed red in the beam of their car headlights. Two couples spotted these creepy peepers while out for a midnight drive near Point Pleasant, West Virginia, U.S.A., in 1966. They claimed the eyes belonged to a birdlike being the size of a man, with giant wings folded over its back, standing off the road near an abandoned explosives factory.

The car's spooked driver hit the gas. With a *whoosh-whoosh-whoosh* of flapping wings, the creature lurched into the night sky and gave hot pursuit. Each time the passengers peered up, the birdman was above them, gliding noiselessly at 100 miles (160 km) an hour. It finally halted its chase when the car reached town.

That was the first sighting of the "Mothman," as the winged monstrosity came to be known, but it wasn't the last. More sightings soon followed. A gravedigger working in a cemetery claimed he was buzzed by a birdman. North of Point Pleasant, a man watched his dog rush into a field to chase something with eyes like "red reflectors." The dog never returned. Fear of the Mothman grew with each sighting. When a bridge connecting Point Pleasant to a neighboring town collapsed in 1967, killing 46 people, some were convinced it was the Mothman's doing. Others believed the Mothman had been trying to warn the town of the disaster. Paranormal investigators speculated that the creature was an alien or supernatural being. It was featured in books and a 2002 movie, becoming a supernatural celebrity.

AGENT JEEPER'S REALITY CHECK

A respected skeptic named Joe Nickell offers an obvious explanation for the Mothman legend. The creature's turf is prime habitat for an oversize owl known as the barred owl, which has large eyes that shine like reflectors. Mistaken for the Mothman, one of these big birds was shot during the Mothman panic of 1966.

Spotting the Mothman is easy today: Just head to Point Pleasant. The town holds an annual Mothman Festival, where you can mingle with eyewitnesses. A statue of the creature stands in a menacing pose in the center of town. True to the legend, its eyes shine like red reflectors.

MORE SPOOKY MYSTERIES

DYATLOV PASS INCIDENT
Investigators blamed a "compelling unknown force" for the deaths of nine Russian skiers in the snowy Ural Mountains in 1959. Their bodies suffered from mysterious injuries, and some of their clothing tested high for radiation!

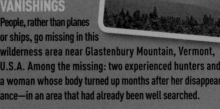

BENNINGTON TRIANGLE VANISHINGS
People, rather than planes or ships, go missing in this wilderness area near Glastenbury Mountain, Vermont, U.S.A. Among the missing: two experienced hunters and a woman whose body turned up months after her disappearance—in an area that had already been well searched.

ROANOKE'S "LOST COLONY"
A group of English colonists arrived on Roanoke Island on the coast of what is now North Carolina, U.S.A., for a fresh start in the New World. Supply ships arriving in 1590 found the settlement abandoned, with few clues to the colonists' whereabouts. The fate of this "Lost Colony" has baffled historians.

EERIE IMAGERY

LES DIABLERIES: Popular in 1860s France, these 3-D photographs of frolicking demons and skeletons are as terrifying as any modern horror movie.

LES ODALISQUES DE SATAN

"HIDDEN MOTHER" PHOTOS: While holding their fussy children steady for primitive 19th-century cameras, mothers would dress as background objects and later crop themselves from the developed picture. Today, the uncropped originals are considered creepy collectibles.

MEMENTO MORI: American families in the 1840s began the curious practice of memorializing deceased loved ones in elaborate photographic portraits. The dearly departed were often posed to look alive. Sometimes, their eyes were even propped open!

Freaky
PHENOMENA

AIIIEEEE! — Mothman

TERRIFYING — Crystal Skulls

SPINE-TINGLING — The Bermuda Triangle

The Bloop Sound

UNSETTLING — ESP

PhEAR FACTOR

PHENOMENA ELICITING ABNORMAL REACTIONS

Agent Jeeper Ranks **PARANORMAL TOPICS.**

CIA

CHAPTER 8

Chill Out

CONGRATULATIONS, BRAVE READER— YOU'VE NEARLY REACHED THE END OF YOUR WILD RIDE THROUGH THE EERIE AND THE WEIRD. By now, you're probably suffering from third-degree goose bumps and an acute case of the creeps. Relax! This chapter is full of fun games and activities that will ease you from the realm of the paranormal to your normal, everyday life. You might even learn how to creep out your friends and family in the process...

SCARES

FACE YOUR FEARS WITH THESE FREAKY PHOBIAS . . .

EVER FEEL UNEASY WHEN YOU SPOT A SPIDER? DO YOU DIG YOUR FINGERNAILS INTO THE ARMRESTS DURING TAKEOFF? It's possible you have a phobia—an especially strong feeling of distress triggered by a specific object, animal, or situation. People afraid of spiders, for instance, suffer from arachnophobia. Fear of flying is aviophobia. But those are garden-variety phobias compared with the more obscure fears people experience. Scan these images and see if any make your heart race and get your skin clammy, then check the list opposite for the official name of each phobia.

7

8

9

10

11

12

13

13

Not everyone thinks 13 is the unluckiest number. People in China, for instance, fear the number four, which in the Cantonese language sounds just like the word for "death." Good luck finding any fourth floors or apartments numbered four in parts of China!

PHOBIA FINDER

1) **COULROPHOBIA** (call-ro-foe-be-ah): fear of clowns
2) **ABLUTOPHOBIA** (ah-blue-tow-foe-be-ah): fear of bathing
3) **ANTHOPHOBIA** (anth-oh-foe-be-ah): fear of flowers
4) **HELIOPHOBIA** (heel-ee-oh-foe-be-ah): fear of sunshine
5) **ORNITHOPHOBIA** (or-ni-tho-foe-be-ah): fear of birds
6) **BATHMOPHOBIA** (bath-mo-foe-be-ah): fear of stairs
7) **LUTRAPHOBIA** (loo-tra-foe-be-ah): fear of otters
8) **CHIONOPHOBIA** (key-on-oh-foe-be-ah): fear of snow
9) **PUPAPHOBIA** (pup-ah-foe-be-ah): fear of puppets
10) **IATROPHOBIA** (eye-at-ro-foe-be-ah): fear of doctors
11) **OMPHALOPHOBIA** (omm-fal-oh-foe-be-ah): fear of belly buttons
12) **CYMOPHOBIA** (sime-oh-foe-be-ah): fear of waves
13) **TRISKAIDEKAPHOBIA** (tris-kai-dek-ah-foe-be-ah): fear of the number 13

BLOOD-SLURPING is best left to vampires, leeches, and the Chupacabra. Everyone else can whip up this sweet recipe that doesn't require draining any veins...

DRiNK
BOGUS
BLOOD!

INGREDIENTS

Light corn syrup   **Water**   **Cocoa powder**   **Food coloring (red and green)**

DIRECTIONS

STEP 1
In a bowl, mix a cup (236 ml) of warm water with ten spoonfuls of corn syrup.

STEP 2
Add two spoonfuls of cocoa powder.

STEP 3
Stir the concoction while adding a few drops of red food coloring. Remember, a little coloring goes a long way!

STEP 4
Drip in a little green coloring for more natural-looking blood.

STEP 5
Let your mix congeal for a bit before applying it to any phony wounds.

Wander around the house offering family members a taste of your scabby snack!

ETHEL THE E.T.'S DISTURBING DATA

A vampire bat slurps so much blood—as much as half its body weight a night—that it has to pee while it drinks, or it becomes too heavy to fly!

GRIM GETAWAYS

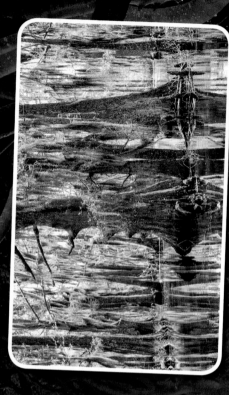

WINCHESTER MYSTERY HOUSE
San Jose, California

Stick close to your tour guide or risk getting lost while wandering this rambling mansion's maze of twisting hallways, stairways that lead to nowhere, dead-end doors, and secret passages. Construction on the house continued around the clock for decades, overseen by a wealthy widow who hoped to confuse the mansion's resident ghosts.

HONEY ISLAND SWAMP
Near New Orleans, Louisiana

Alligators aren't the only creatures said to lurk in this soggy moss-covered wilderness, part of the largest swamp in the United States. Keep your eyes peeled for the legendary Honey Island Swamp Monster, the Bigfoot of the bayou.

HIT THE ROAD
FOR A WILD RIDE
TO THESE
DISTURBING
U.S. DESTINATIONS

EASTERN STATE PENI-TENTIARY
Philadelphia, Pennsylvania

Some of America's most notorious criminals spent their lives locked away in the chilly cells of this harsh prison, which shut down in 1970. Today, brave visitors can take nighttime ghost tours of this happening haunted spot.

INTERNATIONAL CRYPTOZOOLOGY MUSEUM
Portland, Maine

From this mermaid mummy to the Chupacabra, this museum is dedicated to the all-stars of cryptozoology. Be sure to compare your shoe size with plaster casts of Sasquatch footprints.

SONORA WITCHCRAFT MARKET
Mexico City, Mexico

When wannabe sorcerers and practitioners of voodoo run low on supplies, and can't make it to Togo, they come here. The Sonora Witchcraft Market's maze of stalls is stocked with dried bits of unidentified animals, rattlesnake blood, and other exotic spell ingredients.

NEW LUCKY RESTAURANT
Ahmadabad, India

Waiters weave between cement graves in this restaurant built atop a centuries-old cemetery. Why dine with the dead? The owners insist it will bring good luck! (Oh, and the tea is world-famous!)

SEDLEC OSSUARY
Kutná Hora, Czech Republic

Fiendish furnishings—including a chandelier of bones and garlands of skulls—greet tourists who dare enter this small chapel, the final resting place for the artistically arranged remains of more than 40,000 dead.

GRIM GETAWAYS

(CONTINUED)

PLOT THESE GLOBAL SPOTS FOR THE ULTIMATE UNNERVING VACATION

CAPUCHIN CRYPTS
Palermo, Sicily

Hundreds of mummies—some centuries old, many dapperly dressed—lean against walls or sit on benches in the dry, chilly crypts beneath this monastery.

BRAIN MUSEUM
Lima, Peru

Now here's an exhibit with brains—more than 3,000 of them in jars of preserving formaldehyde. This creepy collection of gray matter showcases human noodles that suffered from various medical maladies, along with other oddities.

UP CLOSE AND
CREEPY

Can you identify these six creatures or objects—
all of which were featured earlier in the book—
from their extremely creepy close-ups?

(Answers at the bottom of the page.)

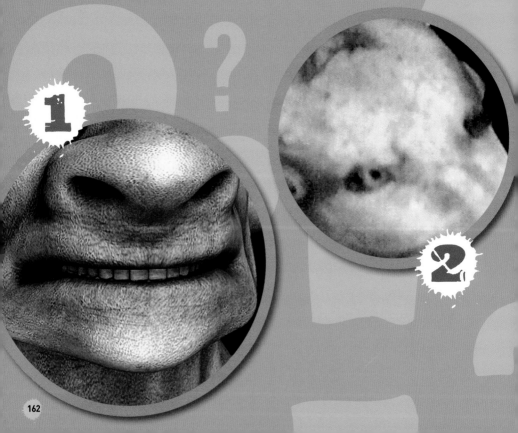

1

2

163

ANSWERS: *1. pukwudgie 2. familiar fish
3. vulture head 4.isobel gowdie
5. blob from above 6. crystal skull*

PHONY Phantom PHOTOGRAPHY

Ghost chasers keep cameras handy to capture all sorts of spooky imagery, from glowing globs of light to human-shaped shadows. Here's your guide to the different types of supposed spectral evidence—and how to fake each kind with camera trickery.

Summon Spooky Subjects for Paranormal Pictures...

VORTEXES: These tiny tornadoes of mysterious mist are thought to transport spirits.

MAKE A FAKE: Wrinkle up a large sheet of cellophane. Flatten it out and keep it in front of your camera's lens while snapping a flash photo. Experiment until you capture a vortex-like image.

ORBS: The least impressive examples of ghostly goings-on, these tiny blobs of light are said to signify spectral activity.

MAKE A FAKE: Most skeptics think orbs are floating motes of dust, so creating them is simple enough. Just kick up some dust in a dark room, then snap a flash picture. The dust will take on an eerie glow in your photo. (Spritzing mist from a water sprayer also works.)

SHADOW PEOPLE: These dark, human-shaped figures lurk in the background of ghost photos.

MAKE A FAKE: If you have a camera with an adjustable exposure time, set it to a 10-second exposure. Mount your camera on a tripod or some other stabilizing surface. Ask a friend to dress in black and pose for the picture. Press the shutter button and count to three, then tell your friend to run out of the picture. The finished photo will sport a spooky shadow person!

APPARITIONS: Images of fully formed see-through specters are highly prized among ghost hunters.

MAKE A FAKE: Use the same exposure-setting technique that captured the shadow person, except have your subject dress in lighter clothes or old-fashioned duds. If your camera lacks an exposure setting, just dab a little moisture on the lens instead. Your subject will have a ghostly glow.

ECTOPLASM: A fluffy smudge believed to represent a wandering ghost.

MAKE A FAKE: Stretch cotton balls into spindly strands, then tangle them in a long clump. Hang all that fluff from a sibling's ear and snap away. Silly String also makes a great ectoplasm stand-in.

Monster Survival

MATCH THE CREEPY CREATURE ON THE LEFT WITH ITS WEAKNESS ON THE RIGHT ...

Guide

ETHEL THE E.T.'S
DISTURBING DATA

Have a vampire on your trail but you don't have the heart to serve him "stake"? Scatter grains of rice or sand across his path. According to folklore, vampires are obsessed with counting tiny things. A pile of rice would keep a bloodsucker busy for hours!

ANSWERS: 1: E. According to modern legend, vampires wither to ashes when exposed to sunlight. Why do you think they snooze in their coffins until sunset? **2:** D. The only way to stop a shambling zombie is to bash its brains. Any heavy tool will do! **3:** B. Scientists have found the beaks of giant squids in the bellies of sperm whales, the "Kraken's" only natural enemy. **4:** A. Bullets and blades won't stop a mummy, but its moldy old bandages erupt in a blaze when burned. **5:** C. Silver bullets are a necessity when hunting werewolves. Their beastly bodies are vulnerable to the pure metal.

167

MONSTER MASH

Which CREATURE Is the CREEPIEST?

LOCH NESS MONSTER

Long-necked Nessie emerges from the murk to pit fins against fur.

BIGFOOT

With his cold glare and unsettling stride, Sasquatch is sure to cinch this cryptid clash.

VAMPIRE

This immortal monster of the night is ready to draw first blood.

WEREWOLF

The full moon brings out the bad side of this ferocious fanged furball.

ZOMBIE

Stinky and starving, this shambling deceased dude is spoiling for a fight!

MUMMY

Does this cursed corpse have the competition all wrapped up?

WITCH

Whipping up a brew of newt's eye and frog's toe, the witch has us spellbound.

CHUPACABRA

The trail of blood from the barnyard means only one thing: The "goat sucker" is on the prowl!

BIGFOOT

Any creature that tries to outcreep Sasquatch has big shoes to fill.

VAMPIRE

The bloodsucking fiend has a powerful thirst, and he doesn't drink to your health.

ZOMBIE

Outcreeping the competition is easy for zombies. They're rotten sports!

CHUPACABRA

Can this hideous, hairless beast lope to the victory circle?

CALLING ALL CRYPTOZOOLOGISTS! Attention all horror hunters! Ethel the E.T. has scoured the seas, forests, and folklore to round up these creatures for a tournament of terror. This isn't a contest of strength or a test of viciousness; it's a showdown to see which monster is best at raising the hairs on your neck and sending tingles up and down your spine. Only one will reign as king or queen of all things spooky! Don't agree with Ethel's choices? Draw your own tournament brackets on a piece of paper and determine your own creepy champion!

And the
CREEPIEST CREATURE
is . . .
THE VAMPIRE!

The other competitors had no shortage of spooky qualities, but it's hard to outdo a monster that sleeps in a coffin and chugs plasma for breakfast.

VAMPIRE

This immortal monster is ready for another meal. Hint: It's not "stake"!

ZOMBIE

Falling to pieces is a good thing in this competition, and the zombie is a pro decomposer.

TERRIBLE TOYS

OUIJA BOARD: Emblazoned with letters and equipped with a creepy pointing device, this mysterious "board game" is billed as a means for communicating with the afterlife. Ask your questions and see where the spirits move your pointer in response.

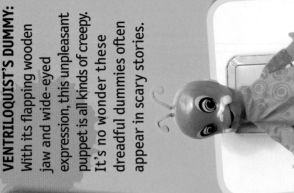

VENTRILOQUIST'S DUMMY: With its flapping wooden jaw and wide-eyed expression, this unpleasant puppet is all kinds of creepy. It's no wonder these dreadful dummies often appear in scary stories.

BLIPPY-IN-THE-MUSIC-BOX: The clowns that pop from normal jack-in-the-boxes are creepy enough. The purple alien that springs from this 1960s toy is the stuff of nightmares!

AGENT JEEPER

Oh, hardy-har. You know I think UFOs are phooey! Now quit foolin' around and follow me back to the CIA. My colleagues have taken an interest in you, Ethel. Ethel...? Hey, where'd she go?

ETHEL THE E.T.

Well, I've gotten all the disturbing data I need for this mission, Agent Jeeper. You have quite the paranormal planet here! Maybe I'll give you a tour of the galaxy next time I drop by Earth. Until then, I gotta fly. Buh-bye!

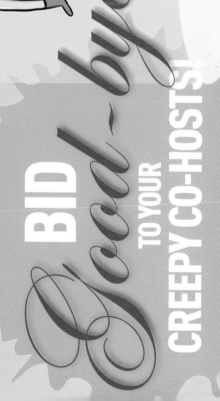

BID *Good-bye*
TO YOUR CREEPY CO-HOSTS!

INDEX

INDEX

CREDITS

Dedicated to Mike Price,
an old partner in paranormal investigations
and a fearless friend in spooky places. —CB

Published by the National Geographic Society
John M. Fahey, *Chairman of the Board and Chief*
Executive Officer
Declan Moore, *Executive Vice President; President,*
Publishing and Travel
Melina Gerosa Bellows, *Executive Vice President;*
Chief Creative Officer, Books, Kids, and Family

Prepared by the Book Division
Hector Sierra, *Senior Vice President and*
General Manager
Nancy Laties Feresten, *Senior Vice President, Kids*
Publishing and Media
Jay Sumner, *Director of Photography,*
Children's Publishing
Jennifer Emmett, *Vice President, Editorial Director,*
Children's Books
Eva Absher-Schantz, *Design Director, Kids Publishing*
and Media
R. Gary Colbert, *Production Director*
Jennifer A. Thornton, *Director of Managing Editorial*

Staff for This Book
Becky Baines, *Project Editor*
James Hiscott, Jr., *Art Director/Designer*
Kris Hanneman, *Senior Photo Editor*
John Foster, Bad People Good Things LLC, *Designer*
Ariane Szu-Tu, *Editorial Assistant*
Callie Broaddus, *Design Production Assistant*
Hillary Moloney, *Associate Photo Editor*
Grace Hill, *Associate Managing Editor*
Joan Gossett, *Production Editor*
Lewis R. Bassford, *Production Manager*
Susan Borke, *Legal and Business Affairs*
Angela Modany and Jacquelyn Stolos, *Interns*

Production Services
Phillip L. Schlosser, *Senior Vice President*
Chris Brown, *Vice President, NG Book*
Manufacturing
George Bounelis, *Vice President,*
Production Services
Nicole Elliott, *Manager*
Rachel Faulise, *Manager*
Robert L. Barr, *Manager*

The National Geographic Society
is one of the world's largest
nonprofit scientific and educational
organizations. Founded in 1888 to
"increase and diffuse geographic
knowledge," the Society's mission is
to inspire people to care about the
planet. It reaches more than 400
million people worldwide each month through its
official journal, *National Geographic*, and other
magazines; National Geographic Channel;
television documentaries; music; radio; films;
books; DVDs; maps; exhibitions; live events; school
publishing programs; interactive media; and
merchandise. National Geographic has funded
more than 10,000 scientific research, conserva-
tion, and exploration projects and supports an
education program promoting geographic literacy.

For more information, please visit
www.nationalgeographic.com,
call 1-800-NGS LINE (647-5463), or write to
the following address:

National Geographic Society
1145 17th Street N.W.
Washington, D.C. 20036-4688 U.S.A.

Visit us online at
nationalgeographic.com/books

For librarians and teachers:
ngchildrensbooks.org

More for kids from National Geographic:
kids.nationalgeographic.com

For information about special discounts for bulk
purchases, please contact National Geographic
Books Special Sales: ngspecsales@ngs.org

For rights or permissions inquiries, please contact
National Geographic Books Subsidiary Rights:
ngbookrights@ngs.org

ISBN: 978-1-4263-1366-0 (Trade paperback)
ISBN: 978-1-4263-1367-7 (Reinforced library binding)

Printed in the United States of America
13/QGT-CML/1